FOR TED & TERE-
MANY BLESSINGS.
LOVE,
"Auntie" Sue

A Tale
of Two Rivers

One Woman's Journey
From the East River to the Târnava Mare

Sue McPhee

Copyright © 2018 Sue McPhee

All rights reserved. This book, or any parts thereof, may not be reproduced in any form, stored in any retrieval system, or transmitted in any form by any means—electronic, mechanical, photocopy, recording, spoken word performance, or otherwise—without prior express written permission of the author. For permission requests, send email to: sue@suemcphee-storyteller.com.

Consumers may order copies of this book by contacting the author at the email listed above or through Amazon.com.

This book is a work of non-fiction. Unless otherwise noted, the author makes no explicit guarantees as to the accuracy of the information contained in this book. The events described are as the author's memory best served at the time of the writing. In some instances names of people and places have been changed or otherwise anonymized to protect their privacy. Author website: suemcphee-storyteller.com

ISBN: 9781731429988

DEDICATION

This book is dedicated to the children of the world. May they inherit what every child deserves: love, safety, nourishment, friendships. They will, after all, be the stewards of the future world, designated caregivers for the generations to come. May we teach them wisely, love them unconditionally, and respect them as we should respect ourselves.

"A hundred years from now it will not matter what my bank account was, the sort of house I lived in, or the kind of car I drove...but the world may be different because I was important in the life of a child." – Dr. Forest E.Witcraft

MY THANK YOU PAGE

This could fill another book! But I will try to be concise.

I want to thank my loving husband, Richard Marshall, who has supported my whims, had patience with my idiosyncrasies, and fully encouraged me to write this book, as did my family, *his* family and my many friends. I thank my sister and brothers who put up with my "craziness" throughout the years and never uttered a discouraging word with regard to my writing. I thank my daughter, Sue, and my son, John, for accepting me for who I am.

I thank my incredible grandchildren: Hunter, Cassie, Madison and Jackson. Thoughts of their lively spirits and unconditional love held me up and kept me going when I just couldn't bear another minute at the computer.

I thank Lauretta Phillips, my friend, mentor, and author of *A Closer Walk* and *Behold Come See Who He Is.* She helped me to believe in myself and gave me words of wisdom when I needed them, as did my friend, Andrea Kaubris, whose boundless positive prodding and cheerleading spurred me on and motivated me to complete this book. I thank Ruth Niven who graciously edited my material. I thank Simon Brooks who gave me encouraging suggestions. I thank all authors and storytellers I have met who hold the beacon of light to lead the way for the perpetuation of story in all its magnificent forms.

Humbly,
Sue McPhee

INTRODUCTION

I wasn't always an adventure-hound. In fact, I was probably the shiest, geekiest and gawkiest kid you'd ever want to meet!

But my life happily and miraculously tumbled into a series of events and circumstances that propelled me into doing things I couldn't have imagined as a kid, even as a young adult or mother. Re-experience with me what some have called riveting, some might call reckless and irresponsible, but most would call, at the very least, "different." I am grateful for the opportunity to bring you to a five year slice of my life, working with infants and children in the ghettos of New York City and the orphanages of Romania.

Two rivers form the backdrop to the events, the emotions, the deep learning that this work brought into my life: the East River in New York City and the Târnava Mare in Romania. The tone of my story runs the gamut from heartwarming to horrifying, from playful to downright funny.

But don't take *my* word for it… Read!

TABLE OF CONTENTS

DEDICATION.. iii

MY THANK YOU PAGE.. iv

INTRODUCTION... v

PROLOGUE... 1
    Romania

CHAPTER I – I WANTED MORE 3
    Leaving the comforts of home.

CHAPTER II – OFF TO NEW YORK CITY 9
    Noise, fear and loneliness: a woman's first encounter
    with the Big Apple.

CHAPTER III –SCHOOL.. 13
    An encounter with the American Academy of Dramatic Arts.

CHAPTER IV – NO LONGER A VISITOR 15
    City immersion.

CHAPTER V – THE GAL FROM THE SUBURBS STAYS
                IN THE CITY............................... 19
    Places to live.

CHAPTER VI – RIVERS 21
    A fascination.

CHAPTER VII – AN INFANT MASSAGE CLASS 23
    Acceptance into new learning.

CHAPTER VIII – SUBWAY FUN 27
    Diversionary tactics.

CHAPTER IX – THE SWEDISH INSTITUTE 31
    Propulsion into a life-changing experience.

CHAPTER X – OFF I GO 39
    Luggage-packing perplexities.

CHAPTER XI – TWELVE WOMEN 41
    Traveling trauma.

CHAPTER XII – THE WORK BEGINS 47
    Orphanages, warehouses, tears and laughter.

CHAPTER XIII - MATERIALISM? LET'S GO SHOPPING! 59
    Shhhh! Don't tell anyone!

CHAPTER XIV – WE MEET OUR MENTOR 61
    One amazing Romanian woman and a whole lot more tears.

CHAPTER XV – WORK TO DO 69
   Unlike any other work.
CHAPTER XVI – SLEEP… PERCHANCE TO DREAM? 73
   Reliving a memory.
CHAPTER XVII – REFLECTIONS ON THE TIMES 81
   "We're not in Kansas, Dorothy….."
CHAPTER XVIII – THE HOSPITAL 85
   Care, cuddling and conversation.
CHAPTER XIX – NO TIME TO REST 91
   So much to accomplish; so little time to do it.
CHAPTER XX – BABIES, BABIES, AND MORE BABIES 97
   "Can I take one home?"
CHAPTER XX1 – PRIVATE HOMES & HOSPITAL VISITS....101
   Motion and emotion.
CHAPTER XXII – STEALING SOULS 105
   Not following the rules.
CHAPTER XXIII – THE BUTTER KNIFE LADY 111
   One opportunity missed… another one embraced.
CHAPTER XXIV – VANS, DANGER, AND REMINISCING... 117
   In harm's way?
CHAPTER XXV – A HOUSE CALL
               WE WILL NEVER FORGET........................ 125
   Get out the Kleenex ……again.
CHAPTER XXVI – THE PICTURE BOOK PROJECT 129
   Preparing a legacy.
CHAPTER XXVII – MIRACLES SMALL AND LARGE 133
   One look of appreciation speaks volumes.
CHAPTER XXVIII – WINDING DOWN: THE RECEPTION... 143
   As if it couldn't get more emotional!
CHAPTER XXIX – GOODBYE ROMANIA 149
   We will never forget you.
EPILOGUE 153
POSTSCRIPT: WHERE ARE THEY NOW? 157

A TALE OF TWO RIVERS

PROLOGUE

I am completely alone.

It is cold and I can't get warm.

I am hungry.

Staring out the window, I watch a matronly woman with a kerchief on her head, plodding along.

She is dressed in drab colors.

The other people have chosen those colors too.

I wonder what is going through their minds today.

It is 1999 and I am in Romania.

CHAPTER I

I WANTED MORE

Such a pretty place, my place of peace and contentment.

So why was I leaving?

Terror washed over me like a Tsunami.

It was just going to be for fifteen days. But this fear!

I could hear my heart pounding inside my head.

Was I having a heart attack? A stroke?

Relax, I thought, you're being silly.

I took one, deep exhale as I rounded the bend at the end of my street. I wanted one last look at the bay, just beginning to come alive. A light frost had covered the vegetation along the water's edge and the morning sun made it glisten.

I could have lingered much longer, watched the light dancing on the waves; the primeval shadows cast by the gulls. But the business of getting myself off to Seattle on time snapped me out of my reverie. I feverishly checked my fanny pack, for about the *seventeenth* time, to make sure my passport was still there, took another deep breath, and headed off for the airport.

It was early October and my head should have been filled with thoughts of pumpkins and falling leaves.

Instead I was leaving my safe, warm and wonderful home for the biggest unknown that I had encountered thus far in my life time.

But I am ahead of myself. Way ahead. This tale begins much sooner.

Back in the mid-nineties, I was a 48-year-old, 16-years-divorced woman; single, but definitely not lonely. Who had time to be lonely? To me, lonely was a wasteful emotion.

In those 16 years, I had finished raising two amazing kids, gotten four degrees, went on several adventures, got certified for scuba diving, had my own radio program for four years, a TV program for two, and landed many diverse and exciting roles in local and city theater and film productions in a medium-sized town in Massachusetts. Boy, was I having fun!

But I wanted more. So in 1994, I moved to Providence, RI, to spread my wings. And spread them, I did. More sophisticated theatre roles, new friends, new jobs, all came at me like an unbridled wind, taking my breath away.

Then, in late winter of 1995, a harbinger of things to come arrived in my mail box in the form of a small booklet. It was from the New England Theater Conference. I mindlessly flipped through the pages during lunch that day and something in the center of the booklet caught my eye. A colorful ad announced that The American Academy of Dramatic Arts in New York City was taking applications and holding auditions for their summer conservatory program.

New York City, I mused. I had never been there. Was it time for another adventure? I had nothing to lose, so I sent in my application, never *ever* dreaming they would respond.

Soon I received a letter stating that my audition was the following month, in Boston. What?

I was so nervous and excited at the same time I nearly threw up! How can I possibly do this? But a little voice in my head kept saying that if this is meant to be, it will be. I trotted off to Boston and did the audition/interview.

I didn't agonize over it. I just plain-old did it!

I had no idea what they were looking for, nor what they wanted, but I did my best.

Then I came home to Rhode Island and went right back to work as if nothing had happened.

As the days passed, I even forgot that I had *done* the audition. Two weeks later, the Academy called to inform me that I had been accepted into the program. They told me my start date and when to arrive. I could barely breathe! Oh my goodness. What do I do now? How will I get there? Where will I stay? Short-term rental? Apartment? Hotel? Some other form of cheap housing?

These questions occupied far too much real estate in my mind for days on end, until I got another phone call. A woman who had somehow discovered that I do intuitive readings called me for some insights. I never found out how she heard about me or who made the referral. None of that became important. Because in the course of our conversation, I learned that she owned a studio apartment in Manhattan. *And* she hardly ever used it.

My heart skipped a beat. I knew it would seem impolite but I risked it anyway. I interrupted the conversation. I was driven, a woman on a mission. I needed to know more about her place. She told me where it was located, the size, and so on. I almost didn't *care* about the details. This might be a place to stay! I shared with her my need for housing in New York City for 6 weeks in the summer. And so, still strangers to each other, we ended up agreeing that I would rent that place from her for a ridiculously low fee of $750/month! *Seriously?*

Now, understand, I was not new to experiencing a sudden coming-together of circumstances when I had a need or an interest or a desire. But this one topped the charts.

So, in June of 1996, I temporarily—so I thought—quit my per diem work in Rhode Island as a physical therapist assistant. I took off, as my late brother would say, "to take a bite out of the Big Apple."

8

CHAPTER II

OFF TO NEW YORK CITY

I had never been there and I was terrified.

At the time, I was living in a beautiful apartment in a safe section of Providence, RI, and subletting two of the other bedrooms. One of my roommates, who had lived in New York City for many years, noticed that I was looking stressed. Truth is, my face was so puckered from worry I looked like my neighbor's bulldog.

My roomie asked me, "Why the dogface?" I was ashamed to admit that my greatest fear was taking the subway. Oh, sure, I was used to the rail system in Boston, but New York City?
Wasn't that where people got killed, terrorized or robbed, every *day*? Indeed, I had seen too many movies.

My roommate laughed and said the one thing I truly needed to hear: "Listen, millions, and I mean *millions* of people take the subway every day and *nothing* ever happens to them."

"Really?" I replied. Then, what was I worried about? I took off for the city, relieved that the odds of my making it out alive had dramatically improved, if only in my mind.
Oh, I was practical. I was cautious, but no longer paranoid.

The apartment that had landed in my lap was lovely, cozy and comfortable. What I had the worst time adjusting to was the level of noise in the city. I had been living in a quiet neighborhood in RI and this was unstoppable noise, 24/7: the traffic, the horns beeping, the squealing brakes and my nemesis: the sanitation department, with that huge trash truck screeching to a stop at every corner at all hours of the day and night.

My sister once asked me why they cleaned the streets and picked up the trash so frequently: "Is it *that* messy?"

It was.

To combat the noise, I slept with both the air conditioner on—even on those evenings that I didn't need it—and the stereo turned up full blast. This got me through the nights.

Days were even more interesting. I learned that I was barely a half-hour walk from the Academy so I walked there every day. I told myself it was because I thought the exercise would be good for me but really I was *still* avoiding the subway.

One day a friend came to visit and we wanted to do some sight-seeing. I hadn't brought my car with me for my New York City stint so I bit the bullet and we figured out the subway system. It was easy!

At that point, I was feeling pretty embarrassed that I hadn't even *tried* this remarkable system that could become my pathway to many adventures. Soon I became a pro, taking myself to auditions and theater events all across town, on the subway!

More friends would come to visit and I became the quintessential New York City tour guide; me, the gal from the suburbs, who thought that Battery Park was where they threw out old dead car batteries and that the East River was still where they threw out old dead gangster-type bad guys in cement boots; me, the grown-up lady who was terrified to step inside a subway.

Yes, *way* too many movies.

CHAPTER III

SCHOOL

The Academy program was great. I loved the variety of classes that were included in that summer semester, most especially the acting class. It was gratifying to learn that in the many years I had been active in local theater productions I had managed to learn *something*.

I didn't exactly shine in the singing class, though. Throughout my entire life it was well-known that I sang like a frog. And in *that* setting I proved that I still did.

Dance and Movement class was fabulous. I had always fancied myself quite the dancer.

Even so, I pretty much stumbled my way through this fairly advanced class without plowing over the obviously more experienced students. But it was during one of those movement classes, as we were stretched out on the floor, doing a breathing and relaxation exercise, that I had some sort of epiphany. It was hard to hold the tears back. I had the most powerful, the most eerie feeling that I was not leaving New York at the end of that summer session, as planned; that I would be there for quite a while; that there was much more for me to experience; and, although I had no idea what that would be, much more for me to do. They were playing the Sinead O'Conner song, *Feel So Different,* during that relaxation session and the lyrics, "I am not like I was before," seemed to burn through my soul, like a branding iron missing its mark.

CHAPTER IV

NO LONGER A VISITOR

I may have been a "chick from the sticks" before I went to New York, but I soon became indoctrinated onto the machinations of the biggest concrete Jenga-land I had ever visited.

I was no longer a visitor. Upon retrieving my car from home and bringing it in to the city, I became quickly enmeshed into the how's and why's of getting around: where to park, where to shop, where to eat. Eat?

During the Academy program, I didn't have an income so I experienced a bit of what it must be like to be a "starving artist." I would walk by the upscale restaurants, smelling tantalizing and sophisticated aromas, watching people enjoy whatever it was that I was smelling. I wiped buckets of drool off my face in those days.

But not wanting to finish the program completely broke, I resisted the urge to indulge in those restaurant feasts and learned how to feed myself on pocket change. I became a master of cheap eats.

There was the little walk-up window where I could get a falafel wrap for a buck and a quarter; the dollar slice of pizza at the corner stand; the 79 cent box of instant mashed potatoes that would serve as two complete meals. I can't believe I really *ate* that stuff, but I did not starve.

The six weeks of the Conservatory program flew by. Just before the program ended, as my thoughts were beginning to turn to packing it up and heading back to Rhode Island, more synchronicities occurred. I had a conversation with someone who said they could get me a "real" paying job. No, this was not going to be in theater or film, much to my dismay. This was a children's hospital that hired physical therapists and physical therapist assistants to provide in-home treatments to infants and children with disabilities. In the blink of an interview, I had a job in NYC and with it the quandary of finding a longer term place to live. My beloved sublet in Greenwich Village was about to end and I was soon to be: New York City homeless.

CHAPTER V

THE GAL FROM THE SUBURBS STAYS IN THE CITY

I was never going to be *totally* homeless because I had made the decision to keep my Rhode Island apartment *and* continue my New York life. Thank goodness for my Providence roommates who helped cover the rent there. And I needed RI as a refuge to go to on weekends when the overstimulation of the city was getting to me.

At that point the whirlwind of synchronicities and serendipities took on a new momentum. Over the next four and a half years, circumstances played out to provide me with short term living situations that were not only cheap but comfortable, congenial and convenient.

As if by magic, I would find one sublet after another, as soon as I would need it.

I *should* say that the sublets found *me*.

Throughout those years, I lived in Brooklyn twice and found three Manhattan living situations that worked out well.

Thank you, Universe!

CHAPTER VI

RIVERS

I have always loved rivers. I love the fast, rushing rivers; the slow, lazy rivers. I love how they snake and wind their way through the countryside and through cities, on their way to ... well, *some*where.

And I've always thought that if rivers could talk, they would have some pretty fascinating tales to tell. I think they hold quite a few secrets too. I got to meet not one but *two* such rivers during those New York City years.

The first one was the fast-moving East River that bordered the East Side of Manhattan. Most of the kids I treated lived in the ghetto sections, New York City Housing tenements, many of which bordered that river. The East River! Remember, I *was* a gal from the suburbs and felt sure that the bottom of the East River was home to all those "dead bad-guy gangster-types" who were fitted with cement boots before they met their demise.

Fortunately, *my* experience with that river was a bit different. There's a highway called the FDR that runs right along the East River and after I got the job working with the children, I learned that I would need to take that highway to get to many of my assignments. Driving down the FDR, you could see boats, bridges and sea gulls, and marvel at the river's fast-moving current. Sometimes you would forget you were in New York City.

Some days, though, I continued to take the subway, and things looked very different down there, deep underground, with all those tracks and trains and people and noises....*and* smells!
You knew for sure you were in a big city.

22

CHAPTER VII

AN INFANT MASSAGE CLASS

I would venture down into that subway many times over the next few years, not just to get to work, but also to get to more auditions and shopping and theater events.

And one day, in the spring of 1999, during the early morning hours, I found myself rushing to catch one of those trains. But I wasn't dashing off to a child's home to give a treatment. I was heading to a class I'd signed up for: Infant Massage Instructor. I'd been looking for this class for a long time. I'd heard and read about its amazing effects. Now I wanted to learn it.

I'd been working in the field of physical therapy for a number of years and had many opportunities to work with disabled infants and children. My training was complete, to a certain extent, but I just wanted to offer *more*.

Flipping through a magazine I had just received in the mail, I found out that they were offering this class in New York City, not far from where I was working!

You couldn't just sign up for it, though. There was a lengthy application form. Several steps needed to be taken before I could even be accepted. Along with the application form, we had to submit two letters: a character reference letter from a health care professional, supervisor, or peer recommending us to the program and also a personal letter we were to write explaining why we would want to learn & teach the Infant Massage Program. This was something I really had to think about. Who do I ask?

At that time, I'd been leading what you would probably call a double life, living half of each week in New York City treating the children and the other half back in Providence, RI. I would truck in to the City for a few days, complete my work with the kids, and then return to RI, where life was a little less hectic yet almost as fascinating.

For this reference letter, I decided to approach a woman from Hasbro Children's Hospital in RI. A tireless woman, she was a Child Life Specialist. Her job was to support children and families through their hospital experience. She became my supervisor after I accepted a four-hour-per-week volunteer position as baby holder and feeder at the hospital, probably the most fun job I *ever* had.

I first met her on my orientation day at the hospital. When she floated through those wards in her ankle-length cotton dresses and tidy aprons, she looked like someone from another world, another time. She made me feel so welcomed, so right at home. "My job here is not always easy, but you won't find one more rewarding." I believed her. Under her guidance, I was soon doing what I had come to do – rocking, feeding, holding the hospitalized babies, taking over for the nurses who needed six hands to perform the endless tasks of the day.

Those four hours were the highlight of my week. It wasn't work. It was pure joy.

So when my supervisor heard of my application to the infant massage teaching program, she was thrilled. She quickly and happily submitted my reference letter.

She had an ulterior motive too, a worthy one. She was hoping that the hospital would allow me to teach the program there after I became certified. What a great idea!

With her reference in hand, there was just one more thing to submit: my personal letter explaining why I wanted to do this. This was the easiest part of the task. I filled three typed pages53 in less than ten minutes and could have gone on to fill four.

It had become clear in my 16-year healthcare career that my work with infants and children was my utmost favorite. I had put my whole heart and soul into it. And although I might have achieved a certain level of expertise, it was the children who taught me well. I couldn't think of a more rewarding, a more exciting way to better my skills than to take this class.

And so it was done. I was accepted into the class.

CHAPTER VIII

SUBWAY FUN

So there I was, on that early April morning in 1999, *very* grateful to be entering that stinky subway station and leaving the cold winds that had been blowing off the East River. I'd gotten quite comfortable riding the subway by then, yet still, when I took a seat on the train that day and tried to relax, I couldn't. I was simply too excited.

So I began to engage in one of *my* favorite little hobbies: people-watching.

Sitting directly across from me on the train was the most adorable child clinging to her mother. She had the biggest, bluest eyes. She'd been fiddling and fussing as small children do, pulling at her coat buttons and swinging her legs. Then she suddenly looked up at me with those eyes and … stuck her tongue out at me!

Well! I was *more* than a little surprised.

But then I realized why. We had been told to bring a life-sized baby doll to class to practice with. And there I was, a grown woman sitting on a subway train, hugging a big baby doll.
I think the little girl was just a tiny bit jealous.

Sitting next to her mother was an old man. I was watching him fall asleep on the train.
His head was bobbing and drifting, bobbing and drifting. Then suddenly it landed heavily on the shoulder of the guy sitting next to him, a rather indignant business man.

They just stared each other down.

Then the old man did something I will never forget. He never said anything. He just looked back and forth, from the business man, to the little child, to her mother, to me.

Then he pointed to his ears. That man had the biggest ears I've ever seen on a human being.

And then those ears started to move, not wiggle or jiggle, *move*, straight up and down, as if they were disconnected from his head!

Well, we all just *stared* at him. And then everyone, including the old man, simply burst out laughing. If there were more of us, people might have thought we were part of a flash mob.

But then the train lurched to a quick stop. I almost dropped my precious "baby." I looked up.

It was my stop. Sigh. My people-watching fun was over–but only for the moment.

CHAPTER IX

THE SWEDISH INSTITUTE

Out in the street, I was exactly where I needed to be. I emerged from the subway and was facing a towering building, an impressive citadel called The Swedish Institute. This was a place that taught different kinds of healthcare programs: medical assisting, nursing, massage therapy.

I arrived at the door armed with a backpack full of books and pens and pencils and notepads and, of course, my life size baby doll. I had named her Shanequa. I have no idea where that came from. It just sort of spilled out of my mouth when I opened the box and I saw her cute little face for the first time.

"What kind of adventure are we going on, Shanequa?"

She never said a word; never complained about the bumpy subway ride. And now we were entering the elevator to ride to the top floor. We found the classroom quickly enough and took our seats with several other women and *their* baby dolls and waited.

Then a woman whose name tag simply said "DIANA" entered the room. She was so cheerful and full of enthusiasm, very well put-together in her fitted suit and beautifully coifed blonde hair. I expected the class to start as soon as she arrived but what happened next fully changed the direction of my life for the next six months.

Diana cleared her throat and began to speak, not of the instruction nor of the lesson plan of the day. She began to speak to us of a medical mission.

It seemed off-topic and I was curious as to why she was telling us all this, but it was fascinating and I found myself riveted, drawn into the drama.

She told us that she had just returned from Romania where she had lead a team of graduates from her most recent Infant Massage Instruction Programs. They were there for fifteen days, bringing the healing and nurturing art of infant massage to the heart-wrenching orphanages.

She spoke of the conditions there and how effective their work had been: more and more fascinating by the moment!

But my mind had fixated on one word, *Romania.* I got the chills when she said it.

I had an odd, inexplicable feeling that I was going there in the not-too-distant future.

Then Diana suddenly switched gears and started the class but I found it increasingly difficult to focus, to concentrate. All I wanted, right then and there, was to know *more* about Romania.

Finally we had a break. I rushed over to Diana and bombarded her with questions. "How can I do this too? When are you going next? Sign me up!"

What on earth was I *thinking*? I had never even left the country. Diana explained that the next organized medical mission would be in six months.

And she emphasized that *now* was the time to sign up and begin the preparations.

"Preparations?" I asked.

She said that there would be background checks and then, of course, shots.

Oh no! Not shots!

She said there would be a few other things too and it would take about six months to complete the requirements. If I accomplished all of that successfully, before the deadline, I could go.

Hmmmm. Preparations. Getting a couple of shots, a background check.

That sounded easy. I had just done *some* of that to get into this class. Piece of cake.

Then the hammer fell. I found out that each selected team member was expected to contribute *three thousand dollars* to defray the team expenses and also purchase new cribs for the orphans. *And* it was expected that this three thousand dollars would be raised through our own *personal* fundraising efforts.

Oh dear. Fundraising. *My* old nemesis.

I always hated asking people for *anything*, even if it was for somebody *else*. It always felt like begging, even if it was for a worthy cause.

I started to sweat. Three thousand dollars? To raise all by myself? No way.

I was nauseous. I was in a daze, yet *still* I found myself asking for the paperwork!

Oh, well yes, my *mouth* was agreeing. My hand was signing the stack of papers. But my mind was in a fog. I felt sick. All I could think was: I can't do this. I can't ask people for *money*. What would they *think*?

But it was too late. By the time my brain and mind caught up with each other, I had already committed to the next mission. Oh boy.

That night, I read the information over and over again. There were hints and suggestions for fund raising; statistics I could use to convince people that indeed this was a worthy cause.

All very nice. I couldn't sleep.

Three days later, I successfully completed the Infant Massage Instruction class.

I should have been happy, ecstatic. Instead I felt paralyzed; paralyzed by this notion of fund raising.

I had to snap out of it. I had to mobilize, call some friends, run it by *them*.

Again, I started to sweat. What would I *say*? They would think I was out of my mind.

Oh, but I *really* wanted to go! So I made that first call, and then another, and another.

Wait a minute. What was happening here? It was easy. Suddenly friends and family members were calling *me* to speak about the mission at their churches and civic groups.

Then I started hosting "bubble gum and balloon" parties at my house. You see, we'd been told that the older orphans just *loved* those gifts. So I made either a bag of balloons or a bag of bubble gum the "entrance fee" to my house parties. And I made it a point to explain to my guests why I was "charging" this.

The results were overwhelming. People not only brought a bag of *each*, they brought money, new baby blankets, toys.

I was doing it. I was fund-raising. I even got a donation of two Polaroid cameras!

You remember those, don't you? They were these box-like cameras where you would snap a picture and out would quickly emerge a square tongue, known as a picture. Then you would wave the picture around trying to get it to dry, thinking that would make the picture develop faster. These two Polaroid cameras were special ones, though. They were called ProCam. The film used in these cameras were designed such that the pictures didn't fade out over time, like the original Polaroids. Dozens of packages of film were donated too, enough to take 700 pictures.

That was another thing we were told about the older Romanian orphans. They *loved* having their picture taken. And these cameras and all that film were going to be an amazing gift for them.

Still, the fund raising was going far too slowly and those three thousand dollars seemed miles away. It was almost time to go and I was in trouble.

Then I made a decision. Going on this mission was far too important to me to let a few dollars get in the way. I decided that, when the deadline came, if I hadn't made the three thousand dollars, if I didn't make my goal, I would just kick in the rest *myself*, empty what was left of my bank account. Wipe it out if I had to.

It was a peaceful decision. No more worrying. But then, as soon as I made that decision, magic happened. The fundraising suddenly took on a new momentum. More and more money came pouring in until three weeks before the trip, when the last contribution arrived, I made my goal. There was nothing left to do but pack and go.

Shanequa stayed home.

CHAPTER X

OFF I GO

Packing for my trip to Romania was interesting.

I hadn't quite checked on what the weather would be like over there. And, well, how much underwear do I really need?

The real challenge was fitting all my personal items *and* the donated goods for the orphans into the two bags they had allotted us. I spent hours cramming and jamming and pushing and sitting on the luggage. Zip; unzip; zip; unzip. Whew!

Broke three fingernails in the process.

Finally fit all the stuff in.

I was a bit more careful with the two cameras, though. I wrapped both of them together carefully in one of the donated blankets; then a second blanket over that; then three, four. It was comical, this big fat bundle.

Those cameras and the film were really the only things I cared about arriving safely. I could live without the underwear.

"Please, oh please, luggage. Don't get lost. Please!"

CHAPTER XI

TWELVE WOMEN

My journey was a bit different than the rest of the team.

We were twelve women in all, and we had to leave the United States in one group. That meant we all had to meet up in Seattle where the mission originated. Eleven of the women came from the West coast. I was the only East Coast gal, so I had the longest trip to make.

By the time I was accepted to go on the mission, I had made some changes to the Rhode Island part of my "double life." I left my Providence apartment and my wonderful roommates and moved my belongings to a home on Narragansett Bay, to live among the seagulls and the tiny houses that lined a cozy little tucked-away peninsula. I was so lucky to find this rental. Apartments were going for a lot more and I stumbled upon this magical place by a quirk of fate. A tiny ad tacked to the bulletin board of a grocery store caught my attention and turned into my ticket to an amazing peace, calm and serenity, a far cry from the New York part of my life.

So it was from this dreamy departure point that I hustled over to the Providence, RI, airport.

I was leaping into the unknown. But there wasn't much time to think about that now. I had to hurry. At the airport, there was the usual morning bustle I would have appreciated more fully had I not been so pre-occupied with the finer details of getting myself and my huge bags full of goodies for the Romanian children checked in on time.

In a matter of hours I had departed that Rhode Island airport, made a quick stop in Chicago, and finally arrived in Seattle. My pulse raced wildly. I had an entire airport to cross via shuttle trains to get to my teammates. With prayers on my lips for the safe transfer of my baggage, I scurried over to the Northwest Airlines gate.

There they were: eleven other women, of various sizes, shapes and ages, wearing the biggest smiles, *and* their Northwest Medical Team T-shirts. Those shirts were our identifying markers so we could find each other. Our seats on that giant jumbo jet were scattered throughout the plane and some of us never even saw each other again until we landed, nine and a half hours later.

As that jet engine roared, I was a bit anxious about exiting U.S. turf.

But sitting next to me was a fellow team member and physical therapist whose life and background were so engrossing, I quickly became lost in the conversation and the spirit of the adventure as we flew up and over the Arctic Circle to Amsterdam.

The flight seemed endless, twelve grey and maroon T-shirts making their way up and down the spacious aisles. We were most definitely conspicuous and drew the curiosity and questions of several of our fellow passengers.

Our brief stint in Amsterdam had its minor pitfalls. A team member had lost her wallet on the plane from Seattle; another team member had not only been very ill, but had taken a serious fall while boarding.

These little mishaps had their quick and successful resolutions, a testament to the resilience of these twelve chosen women. And it was a sort of an omen for the rest of the journey. Potentially not-so-good things would quickly turn to good.

Our departure from Amsterdam was delayed for an hour, we were told, due to "waiting for spare parts." I watched as the expressions on the faces of the other team mates matched mine—a look of profound *worry*. Spare parts?

Our plane finally took off for Bucharest, intact. Two and a half hours later, a safe landing, only to discover that one of my checked-in bags was missing. It was the one with all those collected goodies for the kids *and* the expensive Polaroid cameras and all that film— nowhere to be found!

I was devastated. We filed a lost-and-found claim and hoped for the best. It was all we could do. We had far too much work to get done in the coming days to agonize over it.

Next, we boarded two vans for yet another five-hour ride further north, to our first destination on this mission of mercy: a hotel; a bath; a bed. Oh happiness!

The hotel was, at least, comfortable, although rather primitive. Having travelled over 36 hours, I couldn't begin to describe the kind of exhaustion that overtook me.

But before we could rest, we were told to freshen up a bit as we were to have a meet and greet with our American liaison in Romania whom they called "Papa Chuck."

This very kind gentleman was, at the time, living eight months out of each year in Romania, dedicating his life to building decent orphanages for this country's abandoned children.

He told us to rest up; that we were to be taken the next day to visit some orphanages in that part of Romania.

And so we rested.

As exhausted as I was, as I gathered the blankets up around my chin in that unheated hotel room, I took a few moments to reflect upon my first impressions of Romania.

Physically, except for some of the architecture, we could be anywhere. The terrain resembled the flat farm lands of the United States. We passed by gypsies in wagons. And then buses, slums. I wondered: have I left New York?

An exhausted Sue arrives in Romania.

CHAPTER XII

THE WORK BEGINS

I shut off the light, with dozens of thoughts and feelings invading my soul: anticipation, loneliness, curiosity. Wake-up time was 9:30 am, Romanian time—a lot later than I usually get up. But then again, I was exhausted. The night sounds had lulled me to sleep: some demonstrators singing in the street, lots of car noises, all of which were fairly gone by the light of day. Now Sunday people were in the streets, some dressed for church.

It felt so good to *not* be travelling. As I was getting ready for the day, I could hear a sudden loud commotion going on outside, down in the street. My team mates' voices were chattering like a crowd before a concert. I couldn't figure out *what* was going on. Then, a loud pounding at my door.

"You have to come out here right now! Papa Chuck is here and he wants you to see *you*—right *now*!"

My eyes grew wide. I couldn't figure out why Papa Chuck had singled *me* out like that. I felt like a little kid being called to the principal's office.

So I joined the ladies outside in the street. And sure enough, there was Papa Chuck, arms folded, leaning against a car door. He was grinning like the house cat that slipped out the door.

As soon as he saw me, he turned, opened the back door of the car, and pulled out my lost luggage! Somehow, it had gotten itself on a plane to Zurich. And there it was, contents intact.

We never did find out how many strings Papa Chuck had to pull to get the airlines to find it so quickly, but we didn't care. We cheered and hugged. Now we had the cameras and all that film.

We retreated back into the hotel for a breakfast that was provided by the management: greasy omelets and *very* strong coffee, which we consumed, nonetheless, with gusto.

Gathering with my eleven new sisters in the lobby, our team leader went over the plan of the day. It was a relief to know that this was a well-organized and well thought-out mission.

The two vans we had taken from Bucharest were once again waiting for us, attended by the gracious van drivers, who also served as interpreters throughout the trip.

We traveled for about a half hour to visit the beautiful, modern orphanage that our liaison had just built. The terrain at first was not too unusual, flat as before, with sparse vegetation. It could have been "anywhere, U.S.A." Then the ride became filled with memorable sights. We passed by several houses, some brick; some stucco; most were extremely old with cracks from previous earthquakes. Ghetto-like "apartment" buildings lined some of the streets leading out of the town, clothes hanging from windows and porches, even some graffiti.

Then there were the gypsies and their carts, who stopped our vans once, begging. We thought we'd make them smile by handing out some bubble gum and a few balloons but made a quick departure when they began clamoring for cigarettes.

There was something about the begging gypsies that stirred something in me: a memory. Back in New York City, there was a street corner near a popular coffee shop, not far from my place. I would hustle over there first thing in the morning to get my caffeine fix. There was an amazing old man in raggedy clothes who would stand outside. He was a neighborhood fixture. What a character! Yes, he was panhandling, but he was so *funny* about it.

Most folks would walk right by. Some would throw him a disgusted glance. Others who were quite used to him being there would at least say, "Hi! How ya doing!"

One day, as I was racing to get coffee and get to work, I took a moment to look into his eyes. What I saw stopped me short.

The eyes staring back at me seemed not the eyes of an old homeless man but the loving, peaceful and all-knowing eyes of some kind of unearthly being: an angel?

The people walking by were deliberately *not* giving him money, assuming he'd just spend it on liquor or something else not so nourishing. But standing in line at the coffee counter I couldn't resist buying him his own cup of coffee and a nice big muffin.

I went back outside and he greeted me with a huge smile; no sense of anticipation, no begging, just an honest, from the heart, big smile. Well, that smile got bigger as I handed him the coffee and the muffin and told him, "These are for you." Wide-eyed and the smile growing ever more huge, he couldn't thank me enough. I was so humbled by that moment.

A simple thing, a coffee and a muffin. I could buy that for myself any old time I wanted.

And then there were those eyes, those penetrating eyes. The "angel" looked back at me from out of those eyes. It was a moment I will never forget. It made me think, maybe those angels are everywhere, to remind us, to help us, to create opportunity. I think they're out there waiting to catch you doing a good deed, an act of loving kindness. They might be in the form of a New York City beggar, a loved one, an annoying co-worker, a crying child…or a begging gypsy.

Some of the Romanian gypsies, we were told, lived in their wagons and some lived in small brick huts, several people to a hut. This arrangement was common throughout town as the economy dictated. Electricity was a luxury. Many homes had none. They were simply in the dark, day and night. As we passed by the ones that had lights on, you could see only bare bulbs hanging down to illuminate the interior rooms. Rarely, outside of the hotel, did you see globes or coverings on bulbs.

The newly-built orphanage we visited was a nice surprise though. There were 50 children in Chuck's orphanage, well fed, cleanly dressed, happy and healthy, polite and being educated, so unlike the pictures we had seen of the State–run institutions. The cost to run this place: $7000/month. The funding came solely from out-of-country benefactors. People would choose to sponsor a child and send $25 or more each month to the home. It went directly to their care.

As if things couldn't be more difficult, the Romanian government was not interested in giving them a break on anything and charged them three times the usual cost of electricity, claiming that they are "running a business." They also, up until that time, had given the orphanage a lot of grief. "Why?" we asked, dumbfounded that such a magnanimous venture would be met with such disdain. "Jealousy," our liaison would say. "The government doesn't particularly like the fact that the place is so well run. It makes the state orphanages look bad." And they *are*.

It was an emotional moment when first we joined the children there for our lunch time meal. They sang to us, in such perfect harmony, with no apparent prompting from the adults.
We were touched.

Later that day, we visited two other orphanages, ones that were state-run, a far cry from the scenario we had just left. They were a little beat-up looking on the outside and we don't know what they looked like on the inside. We were only allowed to visit those children in their play yard.

The children there were a bit older than the ones we would be seeing and tending to during most of our mission. They seemed to look fairly healthy.

Conspiring inside the vans to make a "grand entrance," we decided that we would each take handfuls of bubble gum and balloons and step out of the vans carrying the goodies high over our heads. When the children saw us, they swarmed like bees, laughing and squealing, climbing and reaching. Fun for us all! Yet they were a sea of big brown eyes, pleading.

And then we took out the precious Polaroid cameras that had been miraculously retrieved. We took dozens of pictures of the kids. They were really hamming it up. And then we gave the pictures to them to keep. The expressions on their faces, you might have thought it was Christmas.

We stayed and visited with those children for the better part of the morning. Their beautiful faces radiated with excitement and pure joy that we would come and spend time with them. I sensed, too, that they didn't really want us to leave. And neither did we.

Departing from the orphanages, the vans made their way to a warehouse where a container of donated goods from overseas had been delivered. The contents had been removed and were waiting for us to arrive and sort them out.

There were enormous piles of huge, black plastic bags nearly exploding with much needed items: baby blankets, warm children's clothing, knitted goods, some toys. They were all donations that had been collected by previous team members and other benefactors, and had been shipped to Romania in those giant shipping containers. It took six months to arrive.

During that ride to the warehouse, my "sisters" and I were mostly silent, deep in the throes of intense reflection; sorting out, recognizing, and dealing with the emotions of the morning. Later that day, our liaison would tell us that the day care workers at those two state-run orphanages, those rather expressionless women who remained silent, standing in doorways during our visit, were hiding switches behind their backs.

The warehouse visit was yet another overwhelming event. Our job for the next few hours was to open, sift through and begin to organize the goods. But the work was a good diversion for us following the intensity of those orphanage visits.

Dusty and tired, we left some of the work for later in the week and were driven back to our hotel rooms. When we arrived, we were given a brief respite.

Then our liaison told us to "be ready for a surprise." Falling over from exhaustion, we couldn't imagine how our tired and beat-up spirits could handle any more.

But at 7:30 pm we were taken out to a very nice restaurant (yes, they actually *do* exist in Romania): a *heavenly* pizza and pasta place!

Pizza in Romania—tastier and so much more appreciated than the dollar slices I used to bolt down during my "starving artist" days in New York City. We actually drank a tiny bit of beer and wine and were able to relax some.

Back at the hotel, we migrated to our rooms and prepared for another hectic day.

I crawled into bed that night, filled with the energies of those children who have such a vast appreciation for small things. It humbles you; puts a new perspective on the outrageous materialism that we often see in our own country.

Back of a Romanian home.

Crumbling orphanage buildings.

58

CHAPTER XIII

MATERIALISM? LET'S GO SHOPPING!

(Shhhh... DON'T TELL ANYONE...)

Monday morning gave rise to a hustle and bustle that had faded over the weekend. Grey skies and auto lights infiltrated the dawn as we readied ourselves for the day's events. Breakfast was better that day, with fresh cheese and a slice of tomato replacing the previous day's very greasy fare. My stomach was screaming with gratitude.

We were told we were free until almost noontime. Free until noontime? Twelve women set free with a few American dollars that went pretty far in Romania. Materialism notwithstanding, what else were we to do? Veteran shoppers that we all were, we hopped into those vans faster than you can yell the word "sale" and went shopping. They took us to a rug factory to watch the finishing process. It was fascinating to witness. Later we were able to tap into some great bargains. This was gorgeous merchandise at ridiculously cheap prices. I wondered how these people could make a living. I felt guilty doling out small change for an item that should be worth much more. But we were, after all, contributing to their livelihood and that made us feel better.

Finished with the shopping spree, we arrived back at the hotel with a few more minutes to spare so we took *another* quick foray into the local shops; more bargain goodies. Be still my heart. My booty for the day included two small rugs (wouldn't be able to fit *too* much into my bags for the return trip home) and two small vases that reminded me of the Buddhist incense burners that I had back in my Rhode Island house. Once more, the events, items, situations, and even the people conjured up thoughts of my life in the USA.

CHAPTER XIV

WE MEET OUR MENTOR

Bargain hunting done, we piled into the vans and left that town. We were driven an hour and a half north where we would conduct most of the rest of our work. When we arrived, we were greeted by an amazing Romanian woman. She was the person responsible for arranging our many assignments. She was so cheery and bright and energetic. She became our guide, our fearless leader, our support system, in a country none of us knew much about. But as the days passed, we were to learn much about our new mentor.

She was the first to introduce me to the second of the mysterious rivers I met that decade, the river that flowed through her beloved town. On that first day, she pointed to a foot bridge that crossed over the river. "You vill cross de river on dat foot bridge to get to dee orphanage you vill be vorking today."

She was pointing to a very dark but peaceful-looking river that flowed across a field, then away, toward the mountains.

At the top of the foot bridge, I paused. I couldn't resist looking down and wondering what secrets that river might hold. After crossing the long bridge, we still had a 20-minute walk to the orphanage. We passed by fields and factories—factories pouring out smoke and smelly pollution, so close to where the orphaned children lived and played.

We were escorted inside the orphanage, one of the many that were gravely understaffed, and were greeted with another potent smell: 17 toddlers in diapers! Whew-ie!

We immediately changed into our scrubs and were grateful for the many bottles of hand sanitizer we had brought. The children were all sick from one or more forms of influenza and two of the day care workers had Hepatitis A.

We were then brought into their playroom where the children rushed toward us, laughing and reaching out. One child ran right up to my roommate, desperately wrapped his arms around her neck, and clung to her the whole time we were there. The other kids did the same. They were like little sponges, so eager to be just held and loved. It wasn't long before we each had two, three, even four children climbing all over us at once, as if we were a Jungle Gym. The scene was *hilarious*. We were so knee deep and neck high in children we could barely walk!

Some of the toddlers were unable to toddle due to various forms of disability: Down's Syndrome; other birth defects that left a few blind, some unable to stand, walk, or speak. There was also an infant room with 22 cribs, two-by-four feet each, and housed 17 babies. We tried to work with a few but they were very sick and didn't seem to want to be handled or picked up. It was an emotionally difficult time.

For the rest of the afternoon, we worked with the toddlers who were healthy enough, and then we left. We walked quietly back to the parenting center that our mentor ran; back over the footbridge, softly shadowed in the late afternoon sun, again in silence, deep in thought.

That night, as we gathered at the center, we sat at a huge table for our first meal with our mentor. The food was wonderful and looked so lovingly prepared. She sheepishly admitted to running right out the day before to "buy a vegetarian cookbook for her vegetarian visitors."

"I like this," she told us, with a smile on her face. "It's more cheap. I do it more often." Somehow she had gotten the notion that all American women were vegetarians! Little did she know that 10 out of our 12 team members were die-hard McDonald's fans. But we all politely and graciously feasted on the humble plates that were set before us. We later learned that when she was not serving visitors, the typical family fare consisted of pig lard and bread.

During mealtime, we were introduced to her three beautiful children. They were delightful, polite and respectfully interested in our mission. After supper, she began to tell us more about herself. It became clear that she and her family had come through the ranks of serious poverty in this tiny town and now she ran a library across the street that she built with donated funds. She wrote newsletters and bulletins for her church, she ran a women's center, she hosted volunteers like us; all this, while caring for her husband and children. We found out that there wasn't much in that town that she *didn't* do.

We listened to her stories of the dark days of the dictatorship; a time of not so much. We were touched by her humility as she spoke of the past; how Romania was, is, and may turn out to be. She spoke of less-than-adequate living conditions, babies abandoned by mothers, and the economic status of the community. She told us that the average income at that time was our equivalent of 40 dollars a month.

I looked around the room and noticed that many of my team mates were, as I was, having a hard time holding back the tears. It was heavy, intense, but our champion had such a delightful sense of humor about it all, not an ounce of resentment expressed.

Then her voice became soft and quiet; a little giggly and girlish. She looked around to see if her husband was still there and when she knew the coast was clear, she began to tell us of her honeymoon night, the *perfect* girly gossip.

She told how, after the ceremony, they celebrated for hours. Then they went to the house they were to live in. It was very late, midnight.

She admitted she had always been a little shy. But that night, she was downright *terrified*.
She closed herself off in one of the rooms to change into a modest, high-to-the-neckline/down-to-the-floor nightgown.

Then she started shaking with fear. She bolted out of the house as fast as she could. She ran and she ran, nightgown flying in the breeze. Runaway bride, Romanian-style! She ran all the way down to the river, the river that went snaking and winding through the town. She stopped at the river's edge. It was there that she had always felt safe.

She just stood there in the darkness, at the water's edge, shaking. Her sweet and understanding husband had followed her there. He gently took her hand and quietly led her back to their house.

She stopped that story right then and there, but we all figured everything must have turned out ok as she was still with her wise and wonderful husband. And then, of course, there were those three delightful children.

So it was the first of many stories she would tell, late at night, as we sat around the big dinner table, exhausted from our day's work. But this wonderful woman, our mentor, was never tired. She stayed up late every night, plotting and planning and organizing our work, and even paving the way for us, her guests, to have many adventures on this mission of mercy. It was she who told us that in Romania the word "guest" was synonymous with "angel." Well, that just about did it. No more holding back. Out came the Kleenex.

Footbridge we used to cross the river to get to the toddler orphanage.

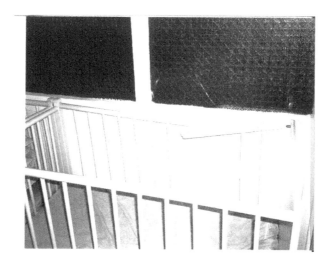

Broken and dangerous cribs inside the orphanage.

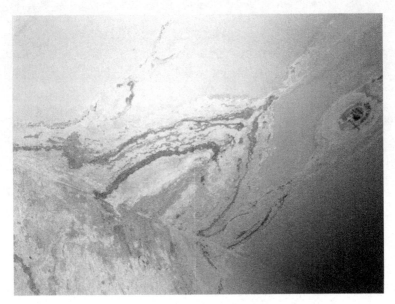

Water-damaged ceiling inside the orphanage.

Toddler orphanage – view of their inadequate play yard.

CHAPTER XV

WORK TO DO

There was still more work to do that evening before we could lay our heads down; more goodies to sort out and store for the mothers we would meet the following day. Our mentor had spoken to us about a tentative plan to cover our remaining days. "Tentative" was *always* the operative word as we discovered that this plan could change dramatically from day to day.

Sorting out all those goodies that had arrived at the warehouse was a challenge. So many bags full of donated items, it made our heads spin. We put sweaters, hats, mittens, blankets all in separate piles, then tried to sort by size. But the real beauty of that experience was marveling at the generosity of all the folks who had taken the time to pack and send these much-needed items overseas so that the children of Romania could have them. We were aware that some of the folks who sent these may have wanted to come over as we did but were not able to. And this was all they could do. But it was in that moment that these generous folks were there with us, if not in body most definitely in spirit.

Upon finishing up at the warehouse we had a brief planning meeting and it was decided that two of us who had physical therapy backgrounds would get together the following day and work on setting up a play group. We would teach some of the local mothers—mothers who had *kept* their children and not left them at orphanages—some therapeutic play ideas while the others were teaching the infant massage classes.

Therapeutic play is often incorporated into infant massage instruction as it encourages healthy growth and development and the two of us were excited to share these ideas.

Finally, finally! We were able to end our work day and stroll back to our home base hotel.

It had gotten very dark. We had been told to stay together as a group, especially if we were out walking at night. And so we did.

There were several young men out in the streets around that time, smoking cigarettes. Most Romanians smoked. Our mentor and her family were exceptions.

That walk became surreal. It was quiet, almost too quiet. Nary an automobile as there *had* been during the day. Eerie.

72

CHAPTER XVI

SLEEP. PERCHANCE TO DREAM?

My head hit the pillow hard that night. And you'd think I'd fall asleep quickly. But in spite of the presence of much needed hot showers, the hotel rooms themselves weren't heated. And even though I pulled those blankets tight under my chin, snuggled as best as I could, my nose was still cold.

I kept tossing and turning for other reasons too. I kept thinking about the orphanages, the children. And *that* made a song pop into my head that I couldn't get out. This particular song comes to me often. It was a song from the '90's, one that those bright-eyed kids in the orphanages reminded me of: *I believe I can fly; I believe I can touch the sky.* *(R.Kelly)*
It played itself over and over again in my head.

Then it occurred to me, while desperately trying to fall asleep, *why* that song haunts me so much. It's because something happened during one of my child assignments back in New York City.

It was an exceptionally cold day in December and I was on my way to visit the children I needed to treat. It was getting closer and closer to Christmas, so I thought I'd wear my Santa's helper hat and give the kids a smile. But it was colder than cold. You'd think with all those tall buildings hiding you from the wind and all those people walking around all at once, almost *hugging* you they were so close, you couldn't *possibly* be cold. But in the winter, the wind off the East River is cold! And I have these pointed ears that stick out. These ears were *freezing* under that silly hat.

So I was more than happy to arrive at a very tall building. Inside, in one of the apartments, lived someone I needed to visit that day, a little girl named Frances.

I pressed on the outside buzzer, hoping it wasn't frozen or broken. The sweet sound of *"bzzzz-zzzzzz"* came wafting through the air and her mother let me in.

Inside, it was warm and cozy and all I could smell were the chocolate chip cookies she had just baked. "Come right on in. Frances has been waiting for ya!"

And sure enough, sitting in the middle of a big sofa—so big she almost disappeared in it—was little Frances. Frances was all of three years old. She had trouble with her legs; trouble standing and walking. Like some of the children we met in the orphanages, she, too, had CP—Cerebral Palsy. But that didn't stop Frances.

Even though her knees were pulled tight together and she could only stand on her toes because her feet wouldn't relax, she would manage to get wherever she wanted to go. She'd grab onto furniture and take herself everywhere. It sure didn't look easy, but she always had a smile and she was always happy.

When she saw me, she got right up off that sofa and climbed her way over to me. She spotted my hat, my pointed ears sticking out, my red nose, my red cheeks. She looked up at me and said, "Sue! You really *are* an elf!"

So we laughed together and I said, "Well, maybe I *am*. At least, for today."

I told her this was the day we would try and climb the indoor staircase to the second floor. She had never done this before. She always had to be carried up and down stairs. But Frances was always eager to try something new. Even things that were difficult to do seemed like fun to Frances. And she was smart. Even though she was only three years old at the time, she knew all the words to all the songs that were on the radio that year. She had a favorite and she would sing it all day. Bet you can guess what it was: "I believe I can fly, I believe I can touch the sky…"

It was the *best* song … for a brave little girl who could barely walk.

So she took my hand and together we went out into the big hallway, over to the staircase.
The stairs were wide with a thick wooden railing. She grabbed the railing with one little hand and *my* hand with the other and she started to climb. One foot, then the other.

It looked *so* painful for her to do. She winced; she took it slow. But she never complained. Instead, she started singing her favorite song. With each phrase, another step. "I believe I can fly" — step, sing—"touch the sky"—step, sing—"spread my wings"— step, sing. And so it went. She kept climbing and she kept singing.

Suddenly it sounded as if there were other voices singing at the same time. I thought I was hearing things. But when I looked up at the top of staircase, peering over the railing were two other little girls. They had come out of *nowhere*.

They had joined her in her song as if to cheer her on. Together they all sounded like a chorus of angels. It was fascinating, but I had to pay attention to what we were doing. I had to make sure Frances was safe.

We kept climbing and climbing. And as we climbed those big stairs, I couldn't resist looking up again and that's when I noticed something odd scratched into the ceiling. I twisted my neck around to see what it was.

Someone had scratched the word "angel" into the ceiling. I was staring at it in disbelief. But again I had to pull my attention back to Frances because now we were getting closer and closer to the top of the stairway. Frances was still climbing and singing, climbing and singing. She sang louder and louder as we got to the top. Finally, she made it.

We both took a deep breath and laughed and hugged, hugged and laughed. She was so proud of herself. She had never climbed stairs before. But on that near-Christmas day, she did.

I looked around for the other little girls, the ones who were cheering her on and singing with her, but they had completely disappeared.

So Frances and I turned and prepared to go down the stairs. But she was looking quite different now. Her little legs had relaxed. Her heels touched the floor for the first time. She stood so proud and tall, full of a confidence I had never seen in her before. As we began to descend, she started singing *again*, louder and louder, "I believe I can fly!"—*screaming* it to the world as if to say "Look at me; look at me!" Going down the stairs. Going down, down, down. When we got to the place where I had seen the word "angel" scratched into the ceiling, I just *had* to look, one more time. I twisted my neck around to look up and it was completely gone. It had disappeared. Just like the little girls.

We kept going down the stairs. Her mother was waiting for us at the bottom. Frances finished her song just as we reach the last stair. Her mother picked her up and hugged her and swung her around. She laughed and squealed. I turned one more time to look up at the stairway. I couldn't figure it out. I couldn't figure out how the girls and the word angel had disappeared like that.

All I know is that it was the happiest day of Frances' life—when we made it to the bottom of those stairs, the two of us. The same two people who went up, came down—a little different, a little changed—the angel and the elf.

Sue and Little Frances

80

CHAPTER XVII

REFLECTIONS ON THE TIMES

The morning alarm snapped me awake so abruptly I fell off the bed onto the cold hard tiles with a thud. My roommate peeled me off the floor and we both started to giggle. "We better go get something to eat before they stop serving breakfast," she petitioned. I was never one to indulge in a morning meal back home, but found it necessary to eat whenever I could find something edible as I was never quite sure what the next mealtime would bring. And we were expending *lots* of physical and emotional energy.

After breakfast, all but two of us headed for the parenting center to engage in the first infant massage class and to prepare layettes to give to the moms. I and one other PT had been asked to hang back and prepare notes for the class we were to present on therapeutic, developmental play techniques.

My teaching partner had gone off to shower now and for the first time since my arrival, I was completely alone. I sat, staring out the hotel window. I was across from the main entrance to some judicial-looking building that might be a court house. A few people in suits and more upscale clothing were hustling in. The red, yellow and blue Romanian flag flew high in the breeze at the end of a tall pole.

I watched a stooped over, matronly woman with a kerchief on her head amble by, a fairly common sight. Although you might see occasional bright colors, most were quite drab, in browns, blacks, greys, muted earth tones.

Although, as our hostess and mentor had told us, the average monthly income in 1999 was our equivalent of around $40/month, 10% of Romania was considered "wealthy." A few were making as much as $5000/month, quite a bit for those times.

After the revolution in 1989, those few were able to take advantage of quick money and were very guarded with it. They didn't feel compelled to help the less fortunate, and instead fled to the coast to spend their money on lavish resorts.

It seemed as if there was no middle class.

The American gentleman who came over and built that beautiful orphanage, as well as his crew, fought the odds and advocated for the orphaned children. There were many areas of Romania much worse than the ones we were able to see on this trip, but, as he told us, "You just can't do everything or help everyone." Thank goodness there were folks like him who at least tried.

My thoughts and emotions, as I sat there alone in the hotel room, ran the gamut from admiration and awe with respect to folks like our American liaison and our Romanian mentor, to isolation, fear and loneliness. You could see it on the faces of the people. Oh, they were cheerful, for the most part; rarely complained; didn't demonstrate resentment; took life as it came.

Yet years of oppression had taken their toll and the old ways were difficult to change. I saw some similarity to ghetto life in New York City: the resignation, the begging, the poverty and sense of futility.

Still there was lightheartedness and frivolity. We heard music in the streets from time to time and saw lovers walking arm in arm.

Our mentor's face was full of sunshine and love, as were the faces of her three children. I was moved by her energy to raise these children and manage to continue her work.

CHAPTER XVIII

THE HOSPITAL

The brainstorming session on the upcoming therapeutic play class went well and we walked back to the parenting center to help out there. On the way, the song that my little "New York City Frances" always sang popped into my head again, only this time it turned out to be another omen. We discovered that arrangements had been made for us to be able to go to the pediatric ward of the local hospital.

More angels? More elves?

Four of us were driven over there to see what we could do to help out. We were soon to be overwhelmingly delighted with what we were allowed to do. Like other facilities in Romania, that hospital was completely understaffed and they were thrilled with any and all volunteer help. So things like rules and regulations, policies and procedures, even licensing requirements—as we have here in the United States—were pretty much thrown out the window.

We had a brief tour of the pediatric building. It had been built as recently as 1986 yet resembled some of the antiquated sanitariums that might have been around in the 30's and 40's in the United States. Hallways were narrow, dark and dismal. The rooms and wards were small.

We were escorted to a room with a sign over the door: "Salon 7." I never did find out what that meant but this was a room where a group of babies were being kept who were not particularly ill but whose mothers had abandoned them there.

The nurse on duty was reluctant to use the word "abandoned," but that is essentially what had happened. We were told it was common. They'd bring the babies in for care, inform the nurse they'd "be right back," and then simply disappear. But it wasn't because they didn't love their babies or want them. They just didn't have money to care for and feed them, and they knew the hospital would provide.

There were six babies in the room that day, each of them in one of those little two-by-four foot metal cribs like we'd seen at the orphanage.

I zoomed right over to one of the babies, all dressed in pink. But she also had this strange "over-wrapping," as did the others. A giant diaper had been wrapped around each of them and they seemed tied and bound by it, once across the chest and once across the pelvis. It allowed for very little movement. They barely turned their heads from side-to-side; just laid there. We weren't quite sure why this was done. Maybe it was the only way they knew. Maybe it was to minimize diaper changing, I don't know. But we had come to work with them, so I started removing her bindings only to be met with a little surprise! *She* was a *he*. The whole group of us laughed and we were grateful for a little bit of comic relief amidst all this intensity.

I worked with this cherub for a while, stretching his arms and legs, massaging his little muscles. We all did the same with the rest of the babies.

It was fascinating to see the beautiful change in them in that short amount of time. They came *alive*. Imagine being released from those bindings. They started stretching and moving around. They looked like little butterflies coming out of a cocoon.

Then a young woman came into the room. She appeared to be somewhere in her late thirties. She wore her long dark hair pulled back tight in a ponytail. She whisked around with a mop and pail—a pail full of nothing but water, plain water—and proceeded to scrub every single thing in that room, including the floor, as if it were the most important work she would ever do. She seemed so upbeat it shamed me. Could I be *that* cheerful if this were my job?

I wanted to speak with her but I knew almost no Romanian and I was pretty sure she didn't know English. Suddenly I found myself blurting out a few words of whatever language other than English I knew: some very rusty French.

"Uh. Bonjour? Comment ça va?" I offered timidly, wondering how stupid I must have sounded. But her eyes lit up. She understood. We started to communicate. I learned that her name was Angela and that she worked there every day as sort of a nursing assistant.

Then, as quickly as she had entered the room, she gathered up her equipment and left. I watched her hustle down the hallway to her next assignment. I'm sure I was unable to hide my disappointment. I wanted so much to continue our chat, but she was busy with *her* work and I with mine. I hoped I would run into her again.

It was tough to leave the babies. The workers there were fascinated with us and the work we had done with them. They were grateful for our donated time and said we could "come back any time!"

At the end of the day, we all went back to the parenting center for dinner. During the evening meal, our warm and gracious mentor and guide made an announcement. She handed us each a folded piece of paper. She said that during the course of our work in Romania, we would inevitably meet and get to know several Romanian women. Each of us was to choose one woman and hand her this folded invitation to a small reception we would have at the end of our mission.

I knew who *I* would invite. And I could hardly wait to tell her: Angela. Angela of the dark hair, sparkling eyes and dauntless enthusiasm. Angela, my new-found French-speaking Romanian friend.

But when? When and how would I run into her again?

Salon 7: the abandoned babies ward.

Slate roof tops: view from the window of Salon 7.

CHAPTER XIX

NO TIME TO REST

I found I needed time to "digest" and process out the emotional impacts of this trip. My team mates and I found ourselves close to the edge of tears so many times. Unfortunately, time was not a luxury we had. There was much to do.

The following morning we needed to get up early so that we could get back to the hospital before 8 AM. We'd been given permission to attend to and feed the babies right after their morning baths.

The night before, another team of women had set up crib toys and mirrors and it was fun to watch the babies' responses. They looked so much brighter and more alert this morning. Also, they were dressed completely differently, in outfits that allowed for more movement. We wondered if our removal of the bindings the day before had prompted the change.

Once again, we looked like a bunch of surrogate moms, holding, feeding and loving these beautiful waifs. These were moments we will *never* forget.

But I couldn't help thinking about Angela. Would I run into her that day? Would I even *get* a chance to hand her the invitation?

I glanced down the hallway and I thought I saw her.

Yes. Yes! When she entered the room, her smile was completely recognizable. It filled the space with warmth and cheeriness.

Again with my bits and pieces of broken French, I handed her the little folded invitation and tried to explain to her what it was. The expression on her face, I will never forget. You might have thought I had given her an invitation to the most exclusive dinner party in all of Eastern Europe.

But the reception was several days away and we still had more work to do.

We returned to the parenting center in time to meet the mothers from the local community who had attended that day's infant massage class. They were all so wide-eyed and eager to practice this loving and healing technique. They were equally fascinated by our little group of American women who decided to interrupt our lives to come to Romania to volunteer our services, on our own dime, leaving family and friends.

After the mothers left, we got down to business again. Our evening had been set aside for unpacking and sorting more of the boxes of donations that had been stored in the warehouse 30 miles away. A truck was scheduled to bring the goods to the center, but had not yet arrived, so we were brought to our mentor's own home just down the road. She apologized for having to take us there in the dark.

We walked, single file, through a dark alley, looking like refugees. Once more— an eerie scene.

Stray dogs barked.

They were a common sight in much of Romania and she warned us to "be careful of that which you step in that creates luck, because I do not want it in my house, thank you."

Twelve soft giggles in the night. Gingerly, we found our way through the somber darkness. Little did we know, we were in for a three hour wait? We frittered away the time looking at her wedding pictures. We chatted with and were entertained by her delightful daughters, two of her three children. We gave each other foot, shoulder, head and hand massages—what *else* would twelve massage people do?—and readily fell into yawning and dozing.

Finally, despite the truck's late arrival, we managed to miraculously perk up and ten minutes was all it took thirteen wired women—twelve team members and one interpreter—to unload the stash of goodies. Unfortunately, one of our team mates caught her ankle somehow and fell heavily to the ground. Fifteen tense and silent minutes passed. We nervously assessed her condition. One of the physical therapists elevated the woman's ankle and I worked with her there on the ground with some visual imagery techniques. After several moments of deep breathing, she finally made an attempt to stand and move about. Success! Outwardly we cheered, but we had received a dope slap of reality in those tension-filled moments. Any of us, at any time on this trip, in this land of grossly sub-standard living conditions and medical facilities, could require emergency medical attention.

Gratefully, we did not.

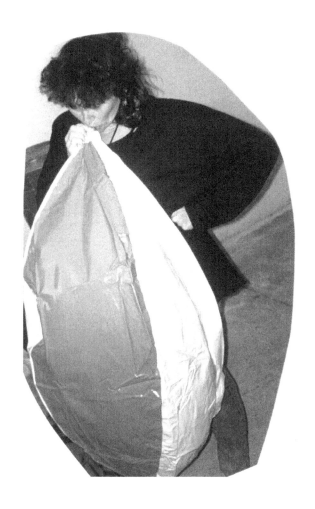

We blow up balloons for the therapeutic play class.

Let's see who has the most hot air. (I think it might be me.) ☺

Yup!

CHAPTER XX

BABIES, BABIES, AND MORE BABIES

The following morning, with ankles intact and energy renewed, we looked forward to the first class that I would team-teach with one of the physical therapists. For an hour or so, we focused on therapeutic play techniques. We showed the mothers in attendance how simple and fun things that can be done in a variety of positions can also help babies develop and have strong muscles and better balance. We made use of the beach balls that were donated and the babies, whose ages ranged from one month to one year, seemed to be having so much fun. So were the moms. Each mom-and-baby team got their Polaroid picture taken engaging in the activities. It was heartwarming to see how much gratitude their faces expressed. I have to say that crossing the language barrier, with or without an interpreter, is an unbelievable achievement. It was a gratifying event, but I couldn't help but feel a gnawing pang for the abandoned children in both the hospital and the orphanages as well as the unfortunate people who would never experience the luxury of this loving, caring method of treatment.

In the afternoon we found an "internet place" where we could rent time on a computer and try to send messages home. This was 1999 and that was a surprising discovery out there in Romania. We sent out what emails we could and then went back to the orphanage to do more work.

Two of us headed into the infant room to assess which babies might benefit from some physical therapy. This was done with an eye toward potentially teaching the daycare givers easy instructions to help the kids. The activities we wanted to teach involved simple positioning, handling, and range of motion techniques to prevent and/or correct contractures, strengthen muscles, and improve balance.

Apparently this particular orphanage had become a "dumping ground" for kids with disabilities. They had appealed to the State several times for them to send a physical therapist over the last two years and none had been sent. The director of the orphanage had spoken with our mentor as well as our team leader about having us go in there to do evaluations and she was thrilled when we all agreed.

The afternoon was, once more, extremely emotional as the children were just begging for love and attention. In this room, there were 17 children to two day care workers. It broke our hearts to see these children want, want, want, and not get.

We're not even sure these children ever got *outside*. How could they supervise them all with that kind of ratio? I never saw any kind of outdoor clothing or appropriate outdoor place to play. I don't know what's worse: NYC ghettos or this place.

CHAPTER XXI

PRIVATE HOMES AND HOSPITAL VISITS

The following day, something different had been arranged: home visits. We split up into small groups. Our mission was to visit local families in their private homes, folks who had just had babies. We wanted to present them with gifts of donated goods.

I was sent off with a vivacious team member from Oregon who was a true delight to be around and, together with one of our van drivers who also helped interpret for us, we visited the home of a cheery young couple who had just had their first child. The baby was four months old and adorable. The home was modest and we were escorted into the bedroom, which doubled as the baby room, kitchenette and living room, not uncommon in this land of such a skewed economic system.

This particular couple was very open with us, eager to share their stories. They had known each other since childhood and went to the same church. They had both had heart wrenching events happen in their lives. Family members and parents had either died from cancer or were killed in a train accident; one was killed in a gas explosion and the young man's disabled brother also passed away at the age of 14. Supporting each other through these tragedies, they had found love and comfort and were beginning this new life together.

They were a stunning couple, she with her long, blonde hair held back in a ponytail and he with his dark, Spanish-looking features. They were very intrigued by our mission and asked to be shown some infant massage strokes, especially ones that relieved colic.

They were eager learners and the little mini-class went well. It was good to know that, once again, we were able to help out. One very big deficit in Romania at that time was lack of access to information of this nature. We were truly setting a precedent.

We all gathered back at the parenting center for lunch. We then had the choice of either working at the hospital or the orphanage. I chose to return to the hospital to work again with the abandoned babies. My favorite little guy—the one we thought was a little girl—was actually returned to his family. We were told: "He'll be back. The next time he gets sick, the mother will just drop him off here again."

And so it goes, so much poverty and inability to care for one's own family. Parents are driven to desperate measures. "My" baby's replacement was a very tiny baby boy with the cutest little elfin ears. We were given no background info, but he looked like he could have been a preemie. I spent my whole time there with him, holding, rocking, singing, walking around, looking out the window, doing a little physical therapy to his very stiff limbs.

We arrived at feeding time and were able to participate. I could only imagine how those nurses were feeling, experiencing five American women helping them out at their busiest time.

CHAPTER XXII

STEALING SOULS

After our hospital visit, we traveled across the river again on the way back to the center. It looked different that afternoon. The wind had picked up. It felt like the same harsh winds that blew off the East River in New York City. In fact, some of the buildings that lined that Romanian river also resembled the ghetto sections of New York where my little patients lived: the clothes hanging from windows and porches, the graffiti.

There were moments in Romania that I felt I had never left New York. And others where I *knew* I had.

There *are* no gypsy carts racing down the streets of New York City, entire families crammed inside, personal belongings dangling off the edges.

I'd heard so much about them when I arrived in Romania: their lifestyle, actually *living* out of their wagons or little huts along the side of the road. They fascinated me.

We had been told to be careful not to try and take their pictures, for if they caught you they might snatch your camera away, might even smash it, so afraid they were that your taking their picture would be stealing their soul.

And I respect that.

BUT!

One day, I was walking down the street with one of my team mates and off in the distance I spotted a horse drawn cart with what seemed to be a gypsy family inside.

The horse was trotting at a clip. And the whole scene was amazing and exciting, with family members clinging for dear life, personal possessions flying off the cart.

I *could not* resist!

I slipped my little camera out of my pocket and crouched face down in the dirt between two parked cars. I poked my head out a couple of times to see where the cart was, and when I thought they were close enough, I leaped out from between the cars, snapped their picture and ran away so fast I nearly knocked over two women and a dog.

I stopped to catch my breath and turned around quickly.

Nobody was chasing me.

Nobody was even *following* me.

Whew! I had gotten away with it.

Later, I whispered an apology to the gypsy family whose souls I may have violated.

But, I got my picture!

Clothes hanging from back porch, Romania

Romanian River we crossed, looking toward the block houses.

The gypsies and their cart.

110

CHAPTER XXIII

THE BUTTER KNIFE LADY

Walking back to the hotel, I didn't figure I would have nearly as grand a photo op as that one, any time soon. But the very next day, we were taken on a van ride through the countryside, as a sort of a break from the intensity of the trip. We headed north to visit a salt mine. It was no longer a commercial mine. Visitors were taken down underground about a half mile, where exposure to the high concentration of closed-in salt air was supposed to have healing effects. People would come from far and wide to do this. They would stay in nearby inns or with local folks, for sometimes two months at a time. They would be taken down into the mine where they would sit for two hours each day, just to breathe in the salt air.

We were told that this treatment seemed to help people with respiratory ailments.

We heard that some of them would even become completely healed.

I wondered if all of the patrons of the salt mine were out-of-country visitors or if the Romanians themselves could also afford this luxury.

So we headed out. Even though it was wet and rainy that day, the landscape along the way was beautiful. I'm really not sure what I expected Romania to look like, but this area had rolling hills with carved ridges, very green, and willow trees cascading over the edges of streams; those red slate rooftops, more gypsies in their horse-drawn carts.

About 13 miles from our destination, one of the vans we were riding in broke down. We pulled over in front of a row of quaint little houses that stood behind one long fence. Each house had a corresponding gate.

Our van drivers stepped out to try and trouble shoot. We watched as they lifted the hood and stood gravely staring at the engine in bafflement, with occasional pointing here and there.

We ladies decided to get out and stretch our legs and at that very moment, out of the gate in front of the house where we had broken down, stepped one of the most captivating characters we saw on that trip. She appeared to be somewhere in her late 70's, but life was harsh there and she could have been much younger. She had a round, lined face, a little scarf tied under her chin.

She wore a dark green cardigan, so tight she could barely button it in the middle, a dark grey skirt down to her mid-calf, old floppy socks and mud-soaked shoes. She smiled at us through a toothless mouth. She just stood there, smiling, with one hand behind her back, looking a bit sheepish and sly, like a cat that swallowed a mouse. All of a sudden she pulled out that hand and we discovered she was wielding a knife!

A butter knife.

She kept waving that knife back and forth in the air, laughing and laughing. She seemed to be getting the biggest kick out of the strange group of foreign women who had landed at her doorstep that day. And you can be sure, twelve cameras came out, snapping away.

And that egged her on even *more*. Posing and grinning.

Then a group of gypsies whizzed past our two sorry vans, laughing and cheering as they sped by. Mortified, the men returned to the task at hand. One of the van drivers knew where we could get some mechanical help, so after they were able to start the van temporarily, we waved goodbye to our spectator, piled back into the van and headed off for the Hungarian part of town. The woman, realizing she was no longer the center of attention, quietly closed the gate and returned to a world we will never know.

Arriving at the mechanic's place was like entering another world. He diagnosed the problem: "a pipe for the fuel-injection was broken." We waited as he attempted to weld the piece together. To get out of the rain and cold, we huddled inside an already crowded garage, around a small wood-burning stove that looked like it had been fabricated from an old oil drum.

The repair was taking longer than expected so one of the drivers offered to take us, in the other *un*broken van, to a nearby cafe "to stay warm and have coffee." So off we went to find adventure in the midst of adversity. The cafe was great, with Cappuccino at 3,000 lei (Romanian monetary denomination) per cup (that's about 18 cents, American!).

But the greater attraction awaited us just outside the café: a Hungarian flea market. So we did what all good women do when waiting for mechanical work to be done: go shopping! While prowling through the beautiful but inexpensive wares, someone heard our American voices and came over to seek us out. His name was Chris, a bright young man from California. He appeared to be about 25 years of age. He had been in Romania for the last 16 months, teaching English in a Romanian school as his Peace Corps assignment. He had much to say about conditions in Romania, describing the entire country at that time as "a complete disaster." He told us that he had about 150 students, only half of whom were fairly teachable and the other half, sadly, he felt, he would simply need to give up on. He said that fifty years of Communist rule had left the people without the ability to engage in critical thinking. The younger generation, being raised in the post-Ceausescu era (after 1989), had only these pre-revolution Romanians as their parents, teachers, guides and role models.

It seemed as if many of the young were destined to become the same. It was Chris's opinion that it would take Romania another solid fifty years to catch up to the rest of the world. From what I had seen, I had to agree.

The van drivers tracked us down as we were having our lively discussion and let us know that the van had been repaired. So we made another stab at making it to the salt mine.

We were eager to see this magical healing place. But because of the van setback, we arrived at the gate too late in the day to be allowed entrance into the mine.

We were disappointed, but hid it well. We did not want our hosts to feel in the least responsible for the way the day had turned out. These gracious people had already gone well beyond the call of duty in seeing to our needs during our stay. It is we who owed *them* a forever debt of gratitude.

So I missed the salt mine experience, but I went home with another prize: another picture … of the butter knife lady.

CHAPTER XXIV

VANS, DANGER, AND REMINISCING

The following day was Sunday and we had our choice of a variety of churches for Sunday service or an option that a few of us eagerly took: an opportunity to sleep in! It was our first real chance to do that since my 37-hour ordeal of getting to Romania in the first place. My roommate and I had already had some opportunities to see the interior of some of the churches and had planned to see others the following week, so we happily chose that sleeping-in option.

Sleeping-in was luscious and, although it's something I rarely do, was so necessary that day. I felt revived.

Lunch at the center was followed by a trip to Sighisoara, an ancient fortress that remains inhabited to this day. We roamed the streets, poking in and out of buildings that shouted history. Camera flashes were abundant as well as amazing "Zen views," and we truly enjoyed our little sightseeing venture. Each van trip always afforded us a chance to see more of the beautiful Romanian countryside. It was fall. The hills were still green and lush, but maple trees were changing colors and shedding their leaves and many of the areas we passed through reminded me of home in New England.

But in our silent times we were processing the depth of this mission, continuously haunted by the voices, sights and smells of the children. Each team member was respectful and supportive of the other's need for quiet moments, a time out, a good cry, to be held and comforted, or left alone to feel the emotional impact of this mission to its fullest extent. Not one team member sought to deny themselves *this* part of the journey; twelve women, on a mission.

Another restful night was followed by a busy day. In the morning, we were split into small groups of two or three with either a driver who could speak English or a driver plus an interpreter. Our mentor had arranged for us to visit local families again, this time focusing on even *less* fortunate ones. My roommate and I were assigned to travel with her and her husband in their van to visit a very poor family in another part of town.

To say that their van was rickety and old was an understatement.

More unexpected adventures surfaced as the van took on a flat tire and attempts to fix it were in vain. So we rode anyway, flat tire and all, in the back section of the vehicle, no seats, bumping along, using the boxes of donated goods to sit on!

We looked like gypsies ourselves as we bounced along, trying to keep from being plummeted across the van and out the back door. Each of us took turns hitting our heads on the ceiling of the van as the streets we had to drive on to get to this family were steep, unpaved, and peppered with incredible ruts. No, *craters.* Our eyes widened even further as they told us of the time when that very same van rolled over and over, down the hill, due to the steepness of the street. We had taken our life in our hands on that van ride!

But we giggled and laughed as both the danger, the adventure and even the humor of it all was not lost on us.

As the van continued to bounce along, my mind drifted back to New York City where the pitfalls and adventures of working in the ghetto were just as numerous, if not more.

With the particular job I had in New York, you didn't get paid if you didn't provide a treatment, even if the treatment was refused or there was nobody home when you went to make the house call. If I had walked six city blocks in the heat of the summer only to find no one there, I wouldn't get paid.

So it was critical that I kept *all* my appointments and saw each of the children. No matter *what*.

One of the challenges to visiting folks in those high-rise NYC housing tenements was that the doorbells didn't always work. You'd get up to the building, take a deep breath, cross your fingers and hope the buzzer wasn't broken. Nine times out of ten, it was broken.

And the rule of thumb, if the doorbell didn't work, rather than walk away and miss an appointment, was that you would wait outside for someone to come out of the building, and while the door was open you'd rush in.

Sounds simple enough.

But sometimes this could take five, ten, fifteen minutes. Your internal meter is running, the clock is ticking, and you've got other kids to see.

One hot summer afternoon, I approached a building and sure enough, the buzzer didn't work. As I stood outside waiting for a fortuitous moment to get in, a gentleman poked his head out from another nearby doorway. He asked, "You tryin' to get in over there?"

I hesitated. I had never *seen* this person before and I wasn't sure what the right or safe answer should be so I just blurted out: "Yes, I need to see someone inside."

He could tell this wasn't a social call. I think my badge and my clip board gave it away.

"Well, you get in over *there* just by comin' in *this* side."

He was holding the door open for me.

I was skeptical, tried to back away. "Really? I didn't know you could do that."

"Yeah, yeah. What you gotta do is climb up the stairs to the roof, cross over the roof, open the door on the other side and there you are!"

"You're kidding." I began to back away even further.

"No, no. People do it all the time." He held the door open even wider, with a broad smile.

I was suspicious, but I was on a mission, just like that day in the rickety van. I *really* needed to see that child. So I went inside as he continued to hold open the door and I started to climb the stairs.

As I climbed, the stair wells got darker and darker. My wild imagination kicked in and I half-expected murderers, thugs and gang members to be lurking around every corner. I climbed and I climbed. Four, five, six flights.

I finally made it to the top stair only to be met with a big heavy steel door. I thought: What if I open the door, step out onto the roof, and the thing slams behind me, leaving me stranded on the roof? I could be hollering and screaming for days before anyone found me up there!

Maybe I'll just go back down and forget the whole thing.

No. No! Duty calls, I argued. I *must* see that child! So I looked around and found a piece of metal I could use as a wedge. Perfect. I'll wedge this thing in the door and if the door to the other side of the building won't open, I can come back here and get back down.

Perfect plan.

I stepped out.

What was I thinking! I was positive there was an axe murderer waiting for me out on that roof. I stepped back. I stayed close to the door.

Then I stepped out a little further and scanned the horizon, a full 180°.

I was casing the joint. When I was sure the coast was clear, I made a mad dash like a Batman outta the movies. It was the best dash a 51-year-old non-running lady could muster up.

I had wings! For a moment, I was Superwoman, Batman, Wonder Woman—all rolled into one! I could hear dramatic suspenseful chase scene movie music playing in my head.

Finally I reached the other door. But it didn't look like the one on the other side of the roof. This one had a doorknob. And, by looking at the hinge, I realized that this one opened inward.

I hesitated but once. Then, I thought, well, if there's a bad guy on the other side of that door, he's gonna get *creamed* 'cuz I'm gonna throw that door open so hard it would knock out the Incredible Hulk. I took a deep breath and turned that knob like my life depended on it—because, after all, I was sure it did.

Success! The door opened. I flung it wide with all my strength, heard the door hit the wall and flew down that staircase; my feet never touched a single stair. Down I went, all six flights of stairs. I reached the apartment door nearly breathless, threw back my shoulders, straightened my shirt, primped my hair, and calmly knocked on the door. "Good morning. I'm here to see Felicia."

No one ever found out what a dangerous adventure I had just been on.

No one knew how I risked life and limb to visit this little girl with the nappy pony tail and teeth as white as a pearl necklace. Just as no one knew how we risked it all that day, pounding down the streets and up treacherous hills in a rickety van in Romania.

124

CHAPTER XXV

A HOUSE CALL WE WILL NEVER FORGET

Happily, we made it to that Romanian house in one piece and piled out of the van with our box of goodies. We were greeted by an amiable young woman, familiarly scarfed and sweatered in tattered greys, with the most winsome smile. She escorted us into a tiny and extremely crowded house. We learned that she and her husband and 10 children (with another on the way) inhabited the three rooms. Beds were large and filled two of the rooms. It was apparent that several of them slept in each bed. Half of the children were home sick that day. We met her oldest, a girl of 10 with radiant, long red hair, dark eyes and freckles. She looked more American than some of *us* did! Her sweet ways and quiet demeanor led us to believe she felt nary a drop of unhappiness or despair. We were drawn into watching her put her books together, pack her tattered knapsack and comb her flowing locks as she prepared to go to school. Her mother, beaming with love and admiration, gently reached over to help her with her hair as she bid her goodbye for the day.

We whose pockets were full of American money; we who wore clothing bought on a whim and stylishly current; we whose tummies were full and seldom knew hunger tearfully watched this joyful interaction. We so wanted to empty our pockets and give, give, give! But, following our mentor's lead, we held back the tears *and* the dollars and respected this woman's dignity.

In that same spirit, we took no pictures. Her humble surroundings, her happy grin, her shy children brought us to a deeper level of awareness. Some of us would pray; some send positive thoughts her way. We would all, at some point, think and weep about this courageous woman.

After we left their house, we were told that this woman would probably continue to have one child per year until menopause, that is, if she didn't die before that. The family's religion prohibited any form of birth control. Our silent response spoke volumes.

CHAPTER XXVI

THE PICTURE BOOK PROJECT

I have always loved picture books. And this was my opportunity to make one myself!

Later that afternoon, my roommate and I prepared ourselves for the work we would engage in for most of the rest of that week. We were to assess, along with the other physical therapist from our team, the physical therapy needs of the children at the orphanage. Our hope was to create a simple plan to help the workers carry out some basic therapy for the kids who needed it the most. I had an idea that we could make a simple picture/instruction book for the orphanage workers to easily follow. We could take pictures of the therapeutic handling and positioning that we felt would most benefit the affected children and write simple captions that would explain each procedure. We would have the captions translated into Romanian by our dauntless interpreter.

So this afternoon became day one of the project.

The orphanage was divided into two sections, one for toddlers and another for the younger babies. My roommate and I concentrated on the older babies, while the other physical therapist focused on the younger ones. Armed with one of the fabulous Polaroid cameras that had been generously donated to us, we proceeded to begin the project. My roommate had the more difficult task of manning the camera. Each time she moved in to take a shot, four or five toddlers would surround her, pulling at her, hugging her, and attempting to stand in front of the camera. It was both funny and frustrating, a joyful task.

The picture book project occupied us for the rest of that day, as well as the following two days. Not every second of our time in the orphanage was spent with the project, however.

We took plenty of time to give each of the children the personal attention they so lacked. You couldn't help but want to do this.

They reached out to you, grabbed you, climbed on you, and loved you. So thirsty for love themselves, they fought their way onto your laps. We loved it!

But underlying the fun and the glee was the stark reality of one burning question: When it came time for us to leave, what would those cherubs have?

132

CHAPTER XXVII

MIRACLES SMALL AND LARGE

The orphanage workers watched our every move with curiosity, and, day by day, they witnessed the small miracles that were happening: the timid child opening up and making her voice heard; limbs moving that did not know movement before; children rolling and stretching in ways they were previously unable to.

I was no stranger to small miracles before I arrived in Romania. I had borne witness to many while fulfilling my physical therapy assignments back in New York City. One of the children in the orphanage, a tiny little girl with shriveled legs and sad brown eyes staring out from a pale and malnourished face, just sat cross-legged on the floor. She made not a sound, no attempt to move. She was so affected that we thought for sure she had been institutionalized since birth. We found out that she had only been dropped off there the night before. What we were able to accomplish with her reminded me so much of one of those New York City miracles.

It was a particularly hot summer day in the city, one where the sun's heat bounces back from the asphalt and makes you feel like bread being baked. And the festering smells from the yet-to-be-picked-up trash creates an odorous cloud that cannot be avoided. My work supervisor had contacted me and asked me to meet her outside of a New York City Housing building, just steps away from the FDR highway and the East River. She wanted to introduce me to my next patient.

I usually worked in, shall we say, the least desirable neighborhoods in the city. This particular building, though, was located on Cherry Street, well-named because, indeed, it was lined with beautiful Cherry trees, a departure from my usual New York City haunts. For some reason the folks here seemed softer, quieter, more reverent, so different from the unhappy neighborhoods I typically found myself in.

When I arrived outside the building, I was greeted not only by my supervisor but also one other woman, a clinical coordinator. I wondered a bit, why this entourage? We rang the doorbell and I braced myself, as I always did when approaching the NYC housing buildings. You never knew what you would find inside. Many were quite run down, unkempt, and on a hot summer day, with no air conditioning, I expected the odors inside might match the ones outside. I was taken aback when a very well-put-together, blue-eyed young lady, in her early twenties, answered the door and invited us in. Her hair was a very light brown, her skin also light. She had a Spanish accent and very politely escorted us into a beautiful living room, furnished with white brocade Victorian furniture, covered with fitted clear plastic to keep it clean and new. The floors in that apartment were so spotless you would feel comfortable having a picnic on them.

There on the floor of the living room, lying on her back, flailing her arms and legs, was her nine-month-old baby girl. We soon learned that the flailing was the only movement the child was able to do. While most nine-month-olds were well past crawling, pulling themselves up to stand, cruising, getting into things, a few even walking, this wee one could only lay there.

It was clear now why all three of us were there. Her needs were many.

As we sat on the floor to make our assessment, her mother politely excused herself for a moment. There was silence. The other two women just looked at me and shook their heads, as if to say, "Don't expect much from this child." I knew quite well the unspoken language of a sinking heart.

But something inside me spoke differently. I just watched and listened. The child had been born with something called "enlarged ventricles," the spaces inside your brain where the fluid flows. Hers were larger spaces than normal, which meant she had less brain matter. Prognosis: poor.

Yet some inner feeling stopped me from having expectations of doom and gloom for this beautiful child.

The women finally left, and week after week, I visited mother and baby. I could see the sense of hope in Mama's eyes. That hope was contagious and we formed a team of two, believing: believing in the child, and the power of a little bit of faith and hard work.

So the mother and I grew close. We trusted each other. She spoke very little of her child's father. I only met him once and I was never told whether he lived there or not. I guessed she was pretty much single-parenting this very affected child. She told me she was born in the Dominican Republic. She must have noticed the curious look I gave her for she further explained that up in the hills of that country were many blue-eyed, light haired and light-skinned people like herself.

In stark contrast to many other households I'd been sent to, this woman was so grateful for my presence. Because of her condition, the baby was allowed a full hour of treatment each time. Mama was so happy to have me there she would escape to the kitchen about halfway through the treatment and reappear quickly with a silver tray. On it there would be a plate with a slice of buttered toast and a small cup of *very* strong Dominican coffee, black, with about six teaspoons of sugar. "It's time for your break," she would say, in her winsome accent. Now, of course, it was against all company rules to accept gifts or food in patient's homes but I knew that her heart would be broken if I didn't accept this little token of her gratitude. And, besides, who would know? The coffee and toast police? So I gratefully downed this tasty token of her unending appreciation.

And *I* was grateful for Maria, for many reasons. Grateful, because she was the only parent who allowed me in her home at nine o'clock in the morning. Most others were sleeping 'til noon!

And, yes, I admit, I was grateful for the coffee and sugar buzz that kept me going throughout my long day in the city.

Whenever I visited there, I had to think creatively. This child was so much more affected than most of the children I had worked with, so much more delayed. I would bring a big ball and lay her, belly down, over the top so she could feel what that was like. There were days she really hated it and let me know! She didn't like touching things and recoiled whenever there was something that felt odd or weird to her. But we persisted, with her mother watching my every move, asking what she could do with the baby to help her along, in between my visits. That was such a refreshing change from the households I normally visited, with parents leaving the room, uninterested in what I was doing nor what they could do to help their child improve. I guess they figured that was my job, even though twice a week was not nearly enough. I guess they were just overwhelmed too. City ghetto life was not exactly stress-free.

And so it went, week after week, visiting the child, drinking strong coffee with her mother, and trying to think outside the box. One day, I spotted a toy at their house. It looked like a tiny swing set with little colorful baubles suspended from a bar. It was meant for a crib. You could lay a child under it and she could reach up and grab the toys.

Well, I'd been trying to get her to sit up, a task most babies could easily do at six months. I decided this toy might help us out. For the next several sessions, I would prop her up, lean her back against me, and have the toy bar in front of her. She could reach forward and as she tried to grab the toys, she could get the feeling of sitting up, all by herself. At least that's what I hoped.

It took four months, but the next time my supervisor stopped by to see how we were doing, there was the baby, sitting up, by herself, laughing and playing. My supervisor was shocked.

How could this happen? But she looked at the mother and I and her look changed to one of calm recognition. She knew that we had both *believed* it would happen.

And it went on. Mama was so patient. And the child soon began to pull herself to standing in her crib. The first day she did that, her mother said to me: "What have you created? She wants to climb right out of that crib!" And we laughed.

That night I had a dream. I dreamt I was walking along the street and mother and child were approaching me. The child was walking, perfectly, and they were both holding hands and swinging their arms. I shared this with Mama and the look in her eyes spoke volumes. She believed the dream was a sign of things to come.

By now, the baby was doing other interesting things too, things that even normally-developing children could not do. On her first birthday, barely able to sit, she could count from one to 10, in both Spanish and English. She got so good at it that you could start anywhere in that line, say "six," and she would finish it for you: "seven, eight, nine, ten!" She sang the entire Happy Birthday song to herself, in both Spanish and English, at the age of *one*. She would hum tunes she heard on the radio. She only had to hear them once and she could repeat the tune, day after day. One day, her mother heard her humming a tune that was new, nothing that had been heard over the radio nor from anyone else. She insisted that the child had invented it. What was so fascinating was that the child even remembered the made-up tune the following day and could hum it again!

And so it went, week after week, for two years, amazing things were happening. The child's mother was so pleased. And, once again, it was summer, hot and smelly, when I got the call that sent chills up my spine. I was pulled off the case. The funding had ended. There was no recourse.

That night, I tossed and turned. How could I tell the mother this? She was so pleased and excited that her child had come this far. She *counted* on my visits.

140

I was allowed just one more. When I arrived, mother and child were outside, walking, just as in my dream. When the little one spotted me, for the very first time, she let go of her mother's hand and ran to me.

Of course, Mama cried when she heard my news. But there was nothing either one of us could do.

I never saw them again. Once we were discharged from a case, we were not allowed to visit or call on them, ever. But I was comforted by the fact that we had done so much together. Mama was now armed with the home exercise routine I had set up as well as her own fortitude, love and tireless drive and I was convinced there would continue to be progress.

That's the hope and faith I *had* to carry away with me, from that New York City apartment, and then again from Romania. I needed to believe that progress would continue.

While we were working on the picture book project, we received such appreciative looks from those orphanage workers. It was those looks that convinced us that these ladies, with the help of our picture book, would carry on the important work.

The three of us who had worked on the project had fun picking out the album and the final pictures that would be placed in it. Then we wrote out the captions, in English, plus a short introductory statement. Thirty-six well planned pictures and statements went into the book, along with a lot of love.

Our interpreter was amazing. She had them all translated in less than an hour!

Project done.

The impact was going to be great. We could all feel that, down to our very souls.

This was the orphanage that had been requesting the State to send them a physical therapist to do evaluations for the past two years. It had been promised, but never happened. With the work that we had done there, as well as the completion of this book, we felt we had at least made a dent in providing a much-needed service.

The child with the shriveled legs who could but sit cross-legged on the orphanage floor? On our last day at the orphanage, she stood up with assistance.

While we were at the orphanage working on the book, other team members were kept busy with various tasks: teaching more infant massage classes to local moms at the parenting center; visiting, holding, hugging, and feeding the abandoned infants in Salon 7 at the hospital; or teaching the infant massage techniques to eager and enthusiastic nurses and aides at the same hospital. I couldn't help but be awe-struck by the enormity and success of the mission. Every team member's contribution to the effort sparked lively conversations at both lunch and dinner each day.

So there we were, the invasion of the American women, swooping through that humble town in Romania, leaving our mark.

CHAPTER XXVIII

WINDING DOWN: THE RECEPTION

Exhaustion hit us like a freight train at a hundred miles an hour. Yet, still, we pushed on. We had to. There was so little time to accomplish so much.

The following morning, we conducted another therapeutic play class at the women's center. We had a crowded house this time. This new set of moms, as all the others had been, were bright, enthusiastic and fun-loving. Pictures were taken; babies smiled; mothers sighed.

By late afternoon, barely able to stand up, we took the opportunity to relax in our hotel rooms for some much-needed rest.

That evening, we prepared for one of the most exciting and emotionally-charged events of the trip. After days of joyous yet heart-wrenching work, our time in Romania was quickly coming to an end and the night of the reception was at hand. I was thrilled when Angela accepted my invitation and was looking forward to greeting and honoring her in that way; honoring her for her good nature, day after day, performing such a difficult job; her hard-driven work ethic, her compassion for the babies. We had so easily hit it off in our communication together: partly Romanian, partly French, a little English, but mostly the universal language of compassion.

There was another reason I was excited about the reception. The day that we missed going to the salt mine, our van driver/guides felt terrible about it. Not wanting us to feel that we had "wasted our day," they took a detour on the way back to the hotel.

We had no idea where we were headed but we were up for adventure. It was clear to us that those van drivers had been wondering how to make it up to us for missing the salt mine. What could possible make American women happy? Aha! You take them shopping! Oh, how right they were. They ended up stopping in a delightful little village known for its flea market that stayed open late.

The highlight of this particular village was, of course, its long row of street vendors with yet another array of tempting yet low priced goods. For about an hour and a half we reveled in the bargains and spent, spent, spent. And just as dutiful husbands might do, the men sat patiently in the vans, occasionally peeking into the vendor huts, amused by our shopping habits.

It was exciting, fun, and challenging as we tried to communicate with the merchants in a variety of languages. I wandered through the tents and tables, marveling at the beautiful merchandise. And it was under one of those tents that I fell in love......with an absolutely gorgeous hand-embroidered outfit! I chose to wear it for the first time the evening of the reception. I tried it on at the hotel and I thought, well, my goodness, I look *Romanian.*

I hustled to join the other women at the reception site. My fellow team mates were already there milling about, waiting for our Romanian guests to arrive.

Angela arrived first and when we spotted each other, we both burst out laughing. Angela showed up looking *very* American, in a silk suit, nylon stockings and high-heeled shoes! We were a sight, the two of us.

The rest of our guests arrived and the chatter began to subside. We sat down to dine and our mentor began with a greeting. Suddenly, a Romanian nurse from the hospital quickly stood up and began a beautiful soliloquy, expressing profound gratitude for the work we had accomplished since our arrival. *Our* work? *Nothing* compared to what these dedicated women did, day after day, year after year. It was humbling to hear her praise *us* in that way.

As if her speech was a cue to the others, one by one, our new Romanian friends followed suit. It was an amazing meeting of the minds and hearts, woman to woman.

Angela and I sat close, in friendship and understanding: two women, worlds apart, who would probably never see each other again. As the night progressed, the meaning of our meeting deepened. We sat in silence. Tears pooled in our eyes.

Then Angela reached for a bag she had been carrying around with her throughout the evening. She handed it to me. *She* had brought *me* a gift. It was a beautiful crystal bowl from her home, probably some cherished item she'd had for years. I knew it would be an insult to refuse it.

My hands shook as they cradled this delicate symbol of our friendship. She had given me so much more than this amazing piece of glass.

The party ended. We said our tearful goodbyes to our new-found friends. And for the last time, twelve women walked in silence, back to our rooms. There was nothing left to say, nothing left to do but pack and go home. But we *were* grateful that we were going to have one more morning with our mentor, one more meal with this hard-working and generous woman.

148

CHAPTER XXIX

GOODBYE ROMANIA

Daybreak was bittersweet. Our last day in Romania.

We arrived at the women's center and were served a wonderful (*vegetarian*, of course) breakfast. We crowded around our mentor and guide, each of us eager to have our turn at taking our final hugs, hugs to this tireless and dedicated woman whom none of us will ever forget.

Our entire team was exhausted, an understatement for sure. But, as always, *she* wasn't tired. And certainly not too tired to tell us just one more story.

As we sat around the big table together for the last time, she told us how, during those dark days of the dictatorship, she had to write her church newsletters and bulletins under cover of night, as this type of freedom of speech was not allowed under the old regime. Even worship itself was banned. After the sun went down, the men would quietly go up into the hills to pray, while she would tip-toe down to the kitchen when she knew the children were asleep.

There, in a corner of the room, on a little table, sat her best friend, teeth gleaming in the moonlight, ragged keys begging to be tapped. Her typewriter. It was old. It was rickety. But she loved her friend dearly. She would sit there for hours preparing her religious material, personal papers and other writings… pretty much anything she wanted.

One night, very close to midnight, there came an ominous banging at the front door. She froze, barely able to breath. She just stared at the door she had forgotten to lock.

Suddenly that door burst open and she breathed a sigh of relief. It was a woman, a good friend from the village. But the woman was crying and crying inconsolably. "They found out about you and what you are doing!" she screamed. "They know about your writing! They are coming to arrest you, put you away for very long time!"

She gently put her hand on the woman's shoulder. "Now it vill be all right. You just go home now. It vill be all right."

The woman reluctantly left.

Now alone, she turned and looked across the room at the one piece of incriminating evidence that could send her to jail, take her away from her beloved family for a very long time: her best friend, her typewriter, sitting there, teeth gleaming in the moonlight.

She slowly walked over to the table and with both hands, scooped up her best friend and held it tight to her belly. She turned and walked out the door that her visitor had left open. She walked and walked, slowly, cautiously, not knowing where she would go or what she would do. She walked all the way down to the river, the river that went snaking and winding through the town.

She stopped at the river's edge, thought of her children and her husband, closed her eyes, took a deep breath, then let go of her friend. She heard the "splash" as the typewriter hit the water, felt the spray hit her face, and knew that her best friend would soon be lying at the bottom in a watery grave. But with head held high, she went home, knowing she would be safe.

That was the last story she ever told us about herself before we left. Many years have gone by since that midnight walk. And she has lived through many things, including the collapse of the regime that forced her hand that night. She eventually got a new typewriter and then even a computer to continue her writing. But none of us could help but notice the wistful look in her eyes whenever she glanced over to the river, the dark and mysterious river that goes winding and snaking through her town, on its way to … somewhere…

EPILOGUE

Leaving Romania, the energy of our mixed feelings, expressed and unexpressed, permeated the air as we headed for the airport. We had a little time to do some sightseeing on the way, but the mood was heavy. We found it difficult to hide our aching hearts. We were abandoning the abandoned! True, we had accomplished much more in our brief mission than we had ever imagined we could. Indeed, we left a legacy. But the soft whimpers of the children, the faces of the struggling people, the stark look of the houses and stores haunted us, even now, in our supposed happy return to our homes and loved ones. It was certainly time to go. Truly, not one of us had a real desire to stay. We *needed* to return home. We *wanted* to return home. But, still, there was that tug. It was a bittersweet tug. It yanked at us as we hustled through the check-in lines and found our way to the gate. Had we really passed through these same gates only fifteen days before? Naïve yet willing participants on a benevolent adventure, we had no clue what was in store. And now, silently marching to our seats for the short flight to Amsterdam, it seemed an eternity had passed.

In Amsterdam, we went our separate ways. Eleven women bid me adieu. Twelve women now possessed the same experience, twelve women deeply affected by the same intense energy. Marked forever, we will never be the same.

I was grateful for the solitude of my journey back to the States. The entrenchment in the team operation had taken its toll and I desperately needed to go within.

I dozed off for a while, dreaming deeply. I woke up with a start as the plane approached Providence, RI. *Was* this all just a dream? Could that entire experience have been real? It seemed like forever, a far distant memory, since I rounded that bend at the end of my road and took a last look at the bay.

But now I was on the flip side of the experience. The plane set down on Rhode Island turf. The strong but gentle arms of my beloved surrounded me and escorted me to the baggage claim area. I'm not exactly sure what I said or did for the next hour or two. I think I was just so dumbfounded to be back. But when we rounded that same bend at the end of my road and I caught a glimpse of the twinkling lights of both the Newport and Verrazano bridges, I wept. Out of the jeep I flew and ran to kiss the ground. Home. Safe.

As the days began to fly by, a word, a song, a feeling would catapult me back to the gravity, the pain, the love, the sorrowful beauty of Romania.

This haunting may wane with time.

But I doubt it.

POST SCRIPT

WHERE ARE THEY NOW?

This has been quite a journey, both the journey itself and the writing about it. It has become all too clear that the story behind writing the story is a story in itself.

In preparation for this book, I spent several years trying to track down some of the folks I met during that period of my life, both for permission to use their name and for this chapter. Time and distance have certainly interfered with this, but this is what has come about:

I found my Infant Massage Instructor, Diana Moore, through Facebook. It was an exciting moment. We ended up having both internet and telephone conversations. In her own words, she is "still very involved in the world of infants." She continues to run her worldwide Infant Massage Instructor Training Courses, but no longer leads any missions to Romania. I have much to thank her for. The bulk of this book would not have been written had I not met her.

After multiple trials, I was finally able to make contact with "Papa Chuck's" daughter. They are both very private people. She told me her father is alive and well and living close to her. He stopped being involved in the Romanian orphanage project back in 2002 and is living a quiet life. She (the daughter) remains involved in helping the young women of Romania.

Our Romanian mentor, that tireless woman who arranged all of our work assignments there (and then some) was equally difficult to find. Hunting around on Facebook as well as Googling her name for years, I miraculously stumbled on a Romanian newspaper that had an ad in it with her full name.

Through Google Translate I learned that the ad was for a workshop she was running for women. The ad mentioned an address that I fully recognized, the location of the parenting center where we had done quite a bit of work. This discovery led to my next challenge: to write her a letter fully explaining why I was writing to her (to gain permission to mention her name in the book). I knew she spoke English (with a thick yet very understandable accent), but I never knew whether or not she read English. So I went on the hunt for someone who could translate the letter. The plan was to send her two letters, one in English and one in Romanian.

At almost the exact time I started my search for a translator, someone commented on one of my Facebook entries about Romania. He actually wrote the comment in Romanian! Turns out he lives here in my home town. I did approach him for the translation. Although he felt quite unsure about doing it as he had not sufficiently used the language in over 40 years, he was willing to at least try. I was more than happy to receive whatever he came up with. It took a while for him to struggle through this task but he did it and both letters finally went out.

I never heard back. Perhaps my letter never arrived. I will never know. But through another visit to the internet, I discovered some YouTube videos that clearly indicate that she and her husband continue to live in the same small town and operate their library and printing company. It appears that she runs workshops for adult women and I see some of the videos where she is surrounded by groups of children. None of the videos, however, provide any means with which to contact her.

I praise and bless her and her efforts. She is a remarkable woman. Perhaps someday I shall receive a return letter.

I also found "little Frances" on the internet as well and we have happily re-united by phone and Facebook. I also got to chat with her mother. They live in the same apartment as they did back in the '90's in Manhattan! It was a bit difficult to find her on Facebook in that she goes by a nickname I never knew about. As of the publication of this book, Frances is 24, a well-spoken, kind and compassionate, deep and thoughtful young woman with a beautiful baby boy. In addition, she is in school as an early childhood education major and manages to find time to work as an advocate for homeless LGBTQ youth in NYC. She is also on the national youth forum for ending homelessness via the Cyndi Lauper True Colors Fund.

Thank you all for being who you are and for letting your true colors shine brightly. I am proud to be here on the planet with you.

As for me, I now live in a log cabin in the woods with my most wonderful husband and life partner who fully supports my many ventures, as crazy as they sometimes are. We are surrounded by beauty and nature, a far cry from my New York City haunts. I still work in the field of massage therapy, I write, I frequently perform my stories, and I continue to marvel at the wonders of the Universe.